From Educated to Employed

FROM EDUCATED TO EMPLOYED

STEPHEN RAE

ISBN (paperback) 978-0-9952396-0-9

Published in Canada

This book is dedicated to my brother,
Donald Andrew Rae

A Note from the Author

A significant portion of my professional life has been spent in varied Human Resource Management roles. These include manager, director and consultant. Primary responsibilities have always included recruiting and coaching. As well as managing recruiters, I have been one.

Over the course of my career I have interviewed thousands of candidates. In fact, I have interviewed hundreds of applicants for entry-level positions. This wealth of experience is distilled into the pages of this manual.

Completing executive search assignments as a consultant has provided valuable insights into recruiting practices. This has helped me understand how organizations manage their interviewing process.

As a community college business instructor, I discovered how much I enjoyed connecting with young adults and creating positive learning experiences. I learned first-hand the concerns and challenges facing graduates entering the workforce.

I found delivering courses, seminars and coaching sessions on finding your first job a personally rewarding experience. This is one of my passions.

This instructional manual is a comprehensive, step-by-step guide. It aims to help you, a new graduate, identify viable and meaningful employment opportunities. And if you diligently follow the steps and strategies outlined in this manual, you will significantly improve your chances of obtaining meaningful employment.

If you are willing to do only what's easy, life will be hard. But if you are willing to do what's hard, life will be easy. ~ T. Harv. Eker

Contents

Introduction xiii

SECTION 1: Overview

The Current Graduate Reality 1

Good News 2

Career Choice 2

Degree = Good Job? 3

Today's Employment Reality 3

You Are In a Big Transition 5

Meaningful Employment 8

The Job Search Method 8

The Career Launch Method 9

About the Manual 12

Getting Organized 13

SECTION 2: Self Discovery ~ Venturing Inward

The Too-Common Scenario 16

Sometimes Luck Works—But it's Not Worth the Risk 17

The Discovery Process 17

Putting it Together 35

SECTION 3: Preparation ~ Laying the Foundation

Branding 38

LinkedIn Profile 38

Other Social Media 46

Resume: To Follow or Lead? 47

Typical Resume Structure 49

Cover Letter 50

Phone Number 52

Email Address & Etiquette 53

Skype or Similar Services...54

Business Cards 55

Attire 56

References and Background Checks....................................59

Self-Management Tools 61

SECTION 4: The Graduate Advantage

Graduate Advantage: What is it Exactly?...........................71

Why Is the Graduate Advantage So Incredibly Important for You?..72

The First Impression 75

Graduate Advantage: The 3-Step Process 79

Digital Interviews 86

Phone Interviews 87

Final Thoughts...88

SECTION 5: Discovering Graduate Advantage Opportunities

Networking...91

Connectors In Person, Online or In Print 93

Preparing to Leave Your Comfort Zone 99

Spontaneous Networking 101

Planned Networking..102

Don't Forget the Paperwork..102

Connecting to a Graduate Advantage 103

SECTION 6: Following Your Resume In

Position Description—What's In It For You 108

The Truth Is: Your Chances Are Slim.................................109

SECTION 7: Pre-interview

Understand the Position..111

Understand the Interviewer, the Company and the Industry 111

Consider Compensation..113

Careers are built on relationships, not on salaries.

Know What Attire is Appropriate 114

Rehearse Your Interview 114

Be Prepared—Small Details Count..114

SECTION 8: The Interview

From the Interviewer's Perspective 115

About Interview Questions 118

A Glimpse of the Interview Process 119

Interviewer Questions...121

Types of Interviews 122

Your Questions..134

Illegal Questions...137

A Word about Psychological Assessments 138

Salary Negotiations...139

Confidence and Enthusiasm 140

The Other Conversation..140

Right After the Interview 141

Summary...143

SECTION 9: After the Interview

The Biggest Mistake...146

A Steep Price 147

Don't Take the Risk..147

Your Reality 148

You Are Now A Different Person 149

Appendices

Appendix I: VIA Character Strengths 153

Appendix II: O'Net Interest Summary 155

Appendix III: Personal Attribute List 157

Appendix IV: Attribute Summary List 159

Appendix V: 11 Transferable Skills Employers Require 161

Appendix VI: Common Transferable Skills Exercise 163

Appendix VII: Common Transferable Skills 167

Appendix VIII: Situational Interview Questions 169

Appendix IX: Traditional Interview Questions 171

Appendix X: Behavioral Interview Questions 175

Introduction

You are standing at the gateway to your future. In your hands, you are holding a key to this gateway. This manual is your key.

After convocation, the already hyper-competitive job market is flooded with ambitious young graduates. You are one of them.

The job market you want to enter is challenging. There are more graduates than jobs, and graduates are competing not only with their peers, but also with grads from previous years. You need to be the one who lands a prized "career opportunity."

There is a lethal myth which can annihilate your chances of launching your career. The myth basically says if you send out enough well-written resumes and covering letters to enough companies, you will land a job. This is a lie.

Here's the truth: You can launch your career if you know what to do. This manual will show you how.

At this point, you can either buy the myth or start using this manual. In the end, chances are the folks who bought the myth will decide to buy this manual. They could have saved themselves time, money and pain.

This manual has its roots in lessons digested from my experience holding human resource managements positions with recruiting responsibilities; teaching business owners and managers how to recruit and interview; interviewing hundreds of candidates for entry-level positions, and many more candidates for other positions; reading way too many resumes; and coaching college students and others on how to launch their careers. (You could say I have been there, done that, and have the T-shirt. In fact, I have a few T-shirts.)

The manual is user-friendly. It is simple and straightforward. The strategies have stood the test of time. The results speak for themselves.

There's a catch. Just reading the manual will accomplish nothing. You have to turn the key; you have to actually do the exercises. You are embarking on a learning journey that is life changing.

The manual starts with a fundamental idea: you have to know yourself before you can understand the types of roles for which you would be best suited. Doesn't this make sense? You have spent at least four years gaining knowledge about different subjects. Before you go any further in life, it's a good idea to learn something about yourself. Learning about yourself is a life-long journey. This manual can help kick-start that journey.

You will learn how to leverage the Graduate Advantage to your full benefit. Consider this your secret weapon which will separate you from millions of other job seekers. This manual provides step-by-step instructions on implementing the Graduate Advantage to access the invisible job market.

By mastering the Graduate Advantage, you can confidently participate in career opportunity interviews. Most graduates are intimidated by even the thought of job interviews. Because of your Graduate Advantage experience, you will look forward to job interviews as the final stage in your successful career launch.

The invisible job market is the source of about 80% of all vacant positions. Once you understand how it operates, you'll be able to clearly see career opportunities and know how to access them.

Job offers are the result of preparation and confidence. But most graduates fear job interviews, fail to do well in them, and end up taking a long time to join the ranks of the employed. But with your Graduate Advantage experience and the information in this manual, your career opportunity interviews will be an easy slam-dunk.

What you accomplish in your career-launch program will serve you throughout your life. The professional relationships you start building now can be a rich source of mutually beneficial satisfaction throughout your career. Your journey of self-discovery, combined with your Graduate Advantage skills, can illuminate your career path through its many twists and turns. It will provide that self-confidence, that deep gut-level knowledge you can do it, and there'll be no stopping you.

Launching your career is one of the most exciting adventures in your life. Enjoy.

Define success on your terms, achieve it by your own rules and build a life you are proud of.
~ Anne Sweeney

SECTION 1:
Overview

Questions to Consider

1. Is this equation still true: Degree = Good Job?

2. Why is this transition so important?

3. What's the difference between a job search and career launch?

Congratulations! The years of hard work have paid off. You have earned your degree. The exams, projects and classes are behind you. It's an accomplishment to be proud of. You are a new graduate, hungry to start your new life.

Perhaps your graduation euphoria is slowly being replaced with the anxiety-producing question, "What now?" Possibly your current financial status needs to be improved—like yesterday.

Maybe you have spoken to graduates from last year's class who are still unemployed. They shared with you how many job ads they have responded to without ever getting an interview.

There is no question about it. There are more graduates than career opportunities. Before I share with you some discouraging numbers, I want to emphasize that you don't have to be part of these numbers.

The Current Graduate Reality

The following stats are often used to illustrate the challenges a new graduate faces:

- One year after graduation, 1 in 2 new graduates is still underemployed or unemployed. That's a lot of graduates.

- Graduates exceed openings by over 30%.

- 47% of recent graduates are still receiving financial assistance from their parents.

- It takes an average of 7.3 months for a new graduate to find employment.

Good News

Companies are still hiring. They are just not advertising their vacancies.

The purpose of this manual is to provide you with a step-by-step method to launch your career regardless of what current graduate reality numbers say.

Career Choice

Your career has a great influence on the nature and quality of your life. It can be a source of healthy challenge, personal fulfillment and economic security. Conversely, if you choose a career that is not a good fit, it can be a source of frustration and disappointment.

According to psychologists, work is usually second only to relationships in determining the quality of your life. Most folks spend a large portion of their waking hours working, including commuting. If you work in a major urban area, you could spend four hours a day commuting to and from work.

A corollary to "work is only second to relationships in the determining the quality of life" is that if your work life sucks (not a Human Resource Management term), your relationships can be negatively impacted.

It's been said that people spend more time deciding what kind of car they are going to buy than deciding what career path they would be best suited for.

Degree = Good Job?

This equation has been the prime motivator for generations to earn a degree. A good job has meant steady employment, job security, and a benefit and pension plan.

The economy started growing after the end of World War II and absorbed graduates as quickly as universities could produce them. Educated meant employed. Life was good. In fact, until the seventies, a degree and a good job were fairly synonymous. About that time, the supply/demand balance started to shift—and not in the graduate's favor. The shift was subtle at first.

Fast forward. The employment market your parents and grandparents knew has morphed into a hyper-competitive, rapidly changing and globally influenced market. This is the market you are entering.

There are career opportunities if you know how to navigate the employment market. The operative word in the last sentence is "if." Not knowing can have a negative reverberating effect on your employment situation for many years to come.

Today's Employment Reality

Prior to the internet (back in the dark ages), the hiring process usually consisted of mailing a resume and a covering letter in response to an ad. This was followed (hopefully) by one or two interviews and some reference checking.

This simple process has morphed into what can best be described as a prolonged assessment process. You can be rejected before you even have a chance to submit a resume. The first thing the hiring manager usually does is Google your name. If they read something they don't like, game over. This is now a common occurrence.

Most organizations have financially recovered from the great recession of 2008–2009. It seems so long ago. However, there has been a reluctance to re-staff to pre-recession levels. This translates into fewer entry-level openings.

Technology used effectively reduces manpower needs. The need for secretaries, accounting clerks and general support personnel has diminished tremendously with the advent of personal computers and related software. On the other hand, new graduates are technologically savvy.

For a number of reasons, Boomers are staying in the work force longer. Some are staying by choice. Others have to stay because of financial obligations or insufficient funding to support retirement. Regardless of the reason, this can limit new-employee hiring.

Community colleges strive to offer employment-relevant courses and programs. Their two-year associate degree often meets the "post-secondary education" requirements of employers. Often community college graduates have lower starting salary expectations than graduates from four-year programs. This translates into more competition for the same entry-level positions.

In a global economy, an organization must be ready to respond to every eventuality. Many companies now maintain just a core group of highly competent employees, and hire people on a temporary or contract basis as the need arises. This provides businesses with manpower flexibility and lower operating costs. However, this reduces the employment opportunities for new graduates.

Experience is a highly sought-after commodity in today's employment market. If you have relevant experience, you have a track record. For the same salary, employers will often choose to hire someone with relevant experience, even if they don't have a degree, over someone with none.

A bad hiring decision can be an expensive misadventure. *Every hiring manager wants to minimize their risk.* Hiring someone with relevant experience helps reduce that risk. Unfortunately, new graduates usually have very little of this prized commodity, relevant experience.

Recent graduates are not only competing with other current graduates, but also with graduates from previous years.

By now you get the picture. There are not nearly enough entry-level opportunities for every graduate.

Most people wouldn't think of starting a whitewater adventure in an old wooden rowboat. Yet many new graduates think they can manage one of the most important transitions of their lives, from graduate to employee, with no self-knowledge or career-launch skills.

You Are In a Big Transition

Transitions are associated with significant life events. These often involve changes to a person's role or surroundings and require a radical restructuring of a person's self-view and world-view. Many of the transitions we experience are just part of the life cycle. With some we have a choice, but with others there are no choices. We can choose to marry and have children. The loss of a loved one or a job is an example of not having a choice.

You are currently in a transition from successful student, as evidenced by your degree, to employee. That's why you bought this manual, right? Some of the characteristics of transitions in a career-launch context are:

They involve hazards & windows of opportunity.

Risks	Rewards
not obtaining meaningful employment	launching your career
taking rejection personally	building professional relationships
unrealistic expectations	gaining real-world experience
stressing out	getting your own place

They typically start with endings. The convocation ceremony officially brings an end to your life as a student, which most people started before the age of six. Gone are the hours of study, lectures, exams and campus life. Your identity as a student has ended.

A variety of possible outcomes are possible, depending on circumstances. In this transition, circumstances play a minor role. You are in control of this transition, if you choose to be. The worst outcome is you give up. Another possible outcome is joining the ranks of the underemployed (a.k.a. malemployed). The best outcome is to quickly find meaningful employment.

They typically span 6 to 12 months, sometimes longer. On the average, it takes a graduate 7.3 months to find employment. You may be thinking, "I have a student loan to start paying back as well as current expenses." Perhaps you have noticed that the Bank of Mom and Dad seems to be losing its investment enthusiasm. Let's remember the operative word in the first sentence is "average." The purpose of this manual is to help you reduce that time.

They involve situational learning. This refers to learning by doing. This manual will explain how to develop and execute relevant skills. You only start learning a skill when you start practicing it in the real world. For instance, you could spend a vast amount of time reading books on job interviewing. Even with all this knowledge and no practice, your chances of excelling in an actual interview are slim at best. Acquiring new skills requires practice. Anyone who plays sports knows the importance of regular practice. The same is true about launching your career.

They involve intrapersonal learning. That is, learning about yourself. In the context of this manual, it's learning about yourself in relationship to work. Not knowing what your strengths, interests and values are, and how they are best used, destroys your chance of finding meaningful employment. Learning about yourself is the process of becoming self-aware. It is fundamental to launching your career.

They involve unlearning. At first, the concept of unlearning something you have learned doesn't make sense. How can you unlearn something? The idea is that when we learn new information about a topic, our paradigm shifts. In other words, we let go of our old understandings and perceptions to make room for new information. Up to this point in your life, learning meant attending lectures and studying. To launch your career requires a different type of learning: situational learning. Prior to graduating, you probably defined yourself in student terms like studious, hard-working and quick learner. Now, as a graduate, you need to understand yourself in terms of strengths, interests, values and possible best-fit career options.

Moving from the known to the unknown is difficult. Your life as a student had a predictable rhythm. This has come to an abrupt end. The excitement of convocation ceremonies can sometimes give way to a host of new feelings. This is probably the biggest change in your life so far.

In leaving school, you are leaving behind a way of life. You may be physically moving to a new location. Probably you are saying good-bye to friends. At this point, you don't know what the future holds.

Your current transition includes major psychological changes including roles, beliefs and attitudes. An important part of launching your career is dependent on learning new roles, beliefs and attitudes.

It is fair to say that moving into the unknown means leaving your comfort zone. There seems to be a correlation between the distance from the edge of your comfort zone, and the ease and speed by which you find meaningful employment.

You are transitioning from an externally based rewards system which has been your compass since kindergarten. In school, you did the work. You were rewarded with marks and promoted to the next grade. As a student, you knew the rules and how to play the academic game. Your degree is evidence of your skill.

Before you become an employee, you must first become a master of the "how to find meaningful work" game. In this new game, there are no external reward systems to mark your progress. Having to reward yourself is going to be one of the most difficult things to learn to do.

Meaningful Employment

For our purposes, meaningful employment is defined as work which aligns with your strengths, values, interests, skills and personality. In an ideal world, there would be a 100% alignment. In the real world there will be trade-offs. The choices you make will determine how they will be aligned.

Self-awareness and authenticity are the cornerstones of meaningful employment.

> *Life is either a great adventure or nothing.*
> *~ Helen Keller*

The Job Search Method

This is by far the most popular method promoted for finding employment. The fact that this method doesn't work for recent graduates doesn't stop recent graduates from using it.

This method uses time-honored tactics, including memorizing an elevator pitch and responding to every employment ad with a standard covering letter and resume.

Some individuals believe that to cover every base you need to utilize the "spray-and-pray" strategy. This strategy takes the traditional job search method another step further, in the belief that if you spray the job market with enough copies of your unsolicited resume, and pray, one of these resumes will generate an interview invitation. Even if no interview invitations are forthcoming (surprise!), you can say you have done everything possible to get a job.

The Job Search Method, including the spray-and-pray strategy, can theoretically work in a rapidly expanding economy where there are many more jobs than job seekers. This is not the case in today's economy.

The Career Launch Method

The Career Launch Method is based on four proven interrelated concepts:

1. *Self-knowledge:* You have to know yourself before you can figure out the type of work for which you are best suited. You have spent years mastering different subjects. Now you must learn about the most important subject of all: yourself. Not in a narcissistic way, but in a healthy, positive way. Learning about your strengths, interests, values and skills as they relate to work is the first step in launching your career.

   In Jay Niblick's book *What's Your Genius*, he tells us about a comprehensive study that has significant importance for career launchers. This study is officially known as the Innermetrix Comparative Performance Study, nicknamed the Genius Project. This study spanned seven years and twenty-three countries and included 197,000 people from a variety of fields. The researchers identified two crucial skills present only in top performers. Those two crucial skills are self-awareness and authenticity.

   Self-awareness means knowing your natural talents: your abilities, innate qualities or aptitudes. These abilities are wired into us at birth and are fully identifiable by age 14. In a broader context, self-awareness includes personality, strengths, values, interests and limitations.

   Authenticity is being who you are, leveraging your self-awareness, and avoiding your limitations as much as possible. Authenticity comes from self-awareness.

   The message is clear. Learning and using these skills can

substantially increase your ability to find meaningful work and excel at it once you have found it.

2. **Face-to-face networking:** Face-to-face contact triumphs over data every time. In other words, when someone meets you they have experienced you. You have made an emotional connection. They will remember you, hopefully positively.

On the other hand, reading about you is just more data. Most people today are drowning in a sea of data. Meeting you and shaking your hand is hundreds of times more powerful than simply reading your LinkedIn profile. Once someone has met you, reading your LinkedIn profile can then professionally elaborate on your background and qualifications.

The Graduate Advantage interview is considered the most effective form of face-to-face networking. Face-to-face networking is about building professional relationships, not asking for a job. Your career-launch activities are built on relationships.

3. **The Graduate Advantage:** Similar to the information interview, this special tool is your career-launch accelerator.

What's the advantage? *You are in a unique position to capitalize on your lack of work experience.*

Chances are, at no other time in your career will people be more willing to help you than they are right now. Everyone has been where you are, looking for that first job and trying to get a foot in the door. You in some way remind every grandparent, parent, uncle or aunt of related offspring; people can empathize with your situation and identify with your struggle. Therefore, most people are willing to help you if you approach them in a sincere and professional way.

The Graduate Advantage is essentially a mini-interview you conduct about career options you are interested in. Once you have mastered the Graduate Advantage, confidently handling job interviews will come naturally.

Research indicates that, on average, 1 out of every 15 Graduate Advantages result in a job offer. Impressive!

4. ***The invisible job market***: Approximately 80% of all available positions are not visible to the untrained eye. This has often been referred to wrongfully as the hidden job market. This doesn't make sense. Never have I requested my staff to "hide" jobs so candidates can't find them—nor have I ever done so myself.

   The "invisible job market" is a career-optics problem. This manual shows you how to dramatically improve your vision.

   There are many reasons why a position is not visible. The following are the most common ones:

   - The company doesn't have the resources to deal with an avalanche of applications.

   - The company did advertise, without success.

   - The position is being filled with a temp.

   - The position's key responsibilities are being shared among several team members.

   - The company hasn't yet decided what to do with the incumbent.

   - No one has gotten around to writing a position description.

   The other 20%, the visible positions, are usually filed by external hires.

Where are all the invisible job openings?

Research has typically shown that Small- and Medium-sized Enterprises (SMEs) have been an important source of new jobs in the economy. Further research has now qualified this even further. Nearly all private-sector jobs have been created by businesses less than five years old. Because they are young, they will naturally be small.

Large, established businesses might not create jobs, but they have job vacancies created by attrition due to resignations, retirements, sickness or death.

For recent graduates, focusing on young, small companies offers the best opportunities for finding meaningful employment. However, for Graduate Advantage, at least initially, be prepared to interview anyone. The Graduate Advantage is as much about practice as it is about obtaining information.

Feedback I've received about small, growing, young companies is usually very positive for several reasons:

- Because they are growing, they are usually looking for "new talent" even if they aren't advertising.

- They are usually open to granting a Graduate Advantage interview if approached professionally.

- Their hiring process is flexible and can be very quick if they see a fit.

About the Manual

This instructional manual is a comprehensive, step-by-step guide. The objective is to prepare you to present yourself professionally to potential employers, and achieve the results you want. If you diligently follow these steps and strategies, you will significantly improve your odds of quickly obtaining meaningful employment.

Two important points to keep in mind:

1. Leaving your comfort zone on a regular basis is fundamental to launching your career. This program won't work if you play it safe. It's as simple as that. To successfully transition from student to employee, you must be prepared to leave the familiar.

2. There is nothing difficult about this program. However, launching your career takes work. You must be prepared to devote 40 hours a week. This can include evenings and

weekends. There is a direct connection between quality time spent, and results produced.

> ***The path to success is to make massive, determined action. ~ Tony Robbins***

Getting Organized

This is one of the secrets to a successful career launch.

You will quickly be inundated with information, notes, draft documents and activity recording. Before you start, I suggest you acquire the free version of Evernote or a similar type of product. Evernote is a note taking, organizing and archiving app. As you work though each section, you can you can keep track what you've learned, documents you are working on, and all your networking activities.

If you find you need more capacity, you can easily upgrade to a paid version. This could be one of the best investments you make in staying organized.

You will find this particularly useful when you are drafting answers to interview questions in Section 8. For each question, you can devote a note (page) to drafting your answer.

If the ladder is not leaning against the right wall, every step we take just gets us to the wrong place faster. ~ Stephen Covey

SECTION 2:
Self Discovery
~ Venturing Inward

Questions to Consider

1. Don't have a clue what to do now you've graduated?

2. Even wonder what you might be good at?

3. Are you afraid an interviewer might say, "Tell me about yourself"?

Self-discovery is a multi-faceted, lifelong journey. Although this section focuses only on learning about yourself as it relates to your career, your work life is interrelated with all other aspects of your life. Work and work-related activities take up to, on average, 60% of your time as an adult. That's a big chunk of time. How are you going to spend it?

The investment you put into learning about yourself now will benefit you for many years to come. And just as importantly, you'll learn about your limitations. Success can sometimes be as simple as avoiding situations where you have to rely on your weaknesses to get the job done.

As a general rule, the more you lead with your limitations, the more you are engaging in career-limiting behavior. By choosing not to learn about your strengths, skills and limitations, you are setting yourself up for potential mental pain and career mal-function.

When an organization hires someone who doesn't operate from

their strengths, no one wins. The organization loses because the individual will never make the contribution the organization expected. The big loser is the individual, whose self-esteem takes a hit, possibly a big one. Without any self-awareness, the employee could be starting on a career path to nowhere.

From a psychological perspective, the effects of not gaining a solid self-understanding have enormous negative implications. These can reverberate throughout a person's career lifespan.

The Too-Common Scenario

All too commonly, an enthusiastic new graduate's career begins with a disconnect between their strengths, skills, interests and values, and the position's performance standards. Usually such individuals simply don't know what they are good at, never mind what their limitations are.

It's hard to watch new employees struggle to make the "fit" equation work. Regardless of how hard they work, they just can't seem to excel. They conclude it must be something wrong with the job. So the natural solution is to get another job. Once again, things don't live up to their expectations. But they just can't put their finger on what exactly the problem is.

Sounds a bit like running on a hamster wheel, doesn't it?

Maybe by the third or fourth job, they have moved up in terms of responsibility. Regardless how far up an organizational ladder they go, their sense of job satisfaction is low or absent. It's that gnawing feeling that something is wrong, but they just can't put their finger on it. By now, the poor career decisions are often having a negative effect on other parts of their lives. This can be fertile ground for what is commonly termed a mid-life career crisis.

I have often been asked if there is any way to bulletproof or ensure a successful career. My answer is always: "It depends." There are several simple and yet critical factors you can choose to control:

- Develop a comprehensive knowledge of yourself.

- Use your self-knowledge, once you've acquired it. This factor is referred to as being authentic.

- Monitor your self-talk. It's possible to be self-aware, work where you use your strengths, and yet "things don't seem to work out." The culprit is often negative self-talk. This is the self-generated, usually silent, ongoing verbal dialogue we have with ourselves.

Sometimes Luck Works—But it's Not Worth the Risk

I feel I was one of the fortunate ones who by "good luck" found some degree of meaningful employment. As a graduate with a major in psychology, I didn't have a clue what I wanted to do. My uncle asked his company's human resource manager what his nephew could do with an arts degree majoring in psychology. The manager's reply was Human Resource Management. The rest, as they say, is history. Over the years I have taken a number of assessments, including an ability test. These combined with my level of satisfaction gained from my various roles confirmed I had made the right choice.

As a new graduate, I lucked out. Unfortunately, I have met too many people who didn't have Mother Luck's blessing.

As a new graduate, you don't have to rely on good luck (or relatives asking human resource managers). This book offers you a practical alternative to good luck.

The Discovery Process

The following exercises may assist you on your self-discovery journey. These are by no means the only exercises, but are some of the ones with which I'm familiar. None of these exercises are mandatory. Do the ones you are comfortable with.

The exercises can be seen as analogous to a jigsaw puzzle: the more pieces connected, the clearer the picture becomes. In a jigsaw puzzle, no one piece is the picture.

As humans, we don't like ambiguity. This sometimes leads individuals to jump to conclusions. One or two exercises, or all taken together, are at best clues—not conclusions.

Exercise #1: Questionnaire

Your answers to the following list of questions may provide you with some clues for further exploration. If a question doesn't make sense or you can't think of a response, skip it and move on to the next one. After you have written your answers in Evernote or a similar app, review them to see if you see any common patterns, strong connections, or new discoveries.

- When you were a child, what did you want to be when you grew up? Why and how has it changed?

- Did your parents have any ideas about the best career path for you?

- What kind of activities did you participate in while growing up?

- What do you have the most fun doing?

- What do other people say you do well?

- Do you prefer to work alone or in groups? Why?

- What do significant people in your life think you would be good at and enjoy doing? Do you agree or disagree with their opinions? Why?

- What is your biggest achievement? Why? How did you accomplish it?

- Of all the jobs you have heard and read about, which ones interested you the most and the least? Why?

- What motivates you the most and least? Why?

- Are you willing to put in long hours and do whatever it takes to get the job done? Why? If not, why not?

- What makes you smile?

- What do you enjoy reading about?

- Who has been the biggest influence in your life?

- What did you enjoy most and least about your educational experience?

- Were there any particular subjects you really enjoyed? Why do you think you enjoyed them?

- Would working outdoors appeal to you?

- Do you see yourself more in an urban or rural environment? Why?

- Describe your ideal employer. Here are some questions which might help you:

  - Are they an international conglomerate or a regional player?

  - What are their products or services?

  - What are they known for?

  - What would their employees say about them?

  - Are they a new company or have they been around for a long time?

  - Describe your boss. How would you know he or she would be a good boss for you?

- Describe the environment you are working in.

- How are you spending most of your time on an average day?

- Do you see yourself more as an introvert or an extrovert?

- What do you like to talk about?

- What sort of things do you want to learn in the future?

- On a scale of 1 to 10, how comfortable are you with ambiguity?

Exercise #2: Career Wheel

A career wheel is used to help bring clarity to an individual's career exploration activities. A career wheel is a visual representation of the different factors which can impact your career option choices. It's another source of possible clues. The wheel is composed of different sections, often 8, with different factors.

The Highlands Company's *Personal Vision Wheel* is an example of a career wheel.

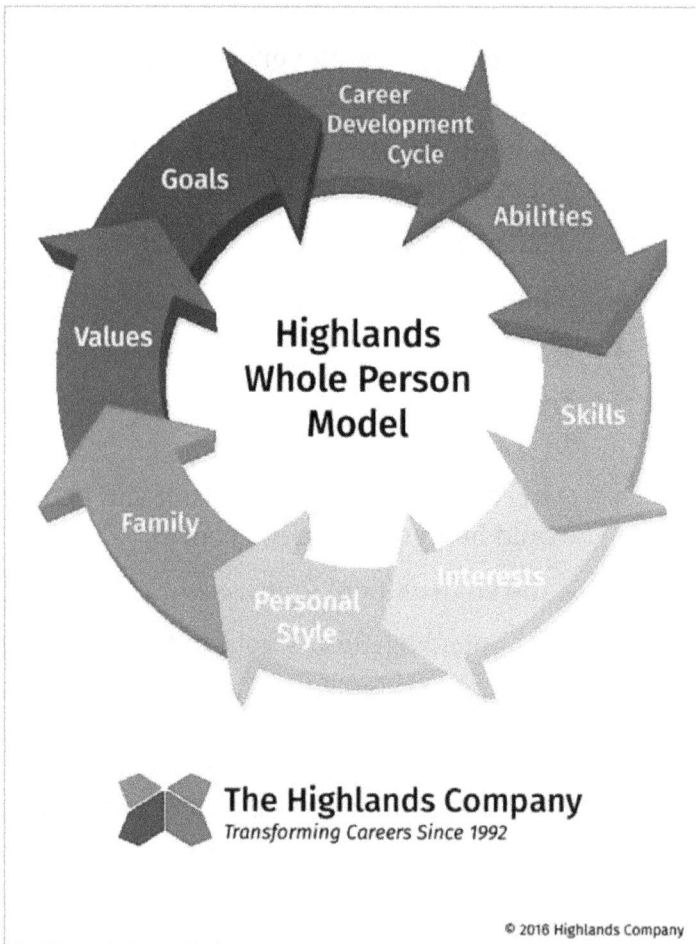

The Highlands Company
Transforming Careers Since 1992

© 2016 Highlands Company

Career development cycle: understanding life transitions

- view work life as going through stages of development similar to personal life
- focus is on stages of career development rather than specific ages

Natural abilities: innate strengths; how one is hard wired

- don't improve with practice or go away with neglect
- remain stable throughout work life (unlike interests and personalities)

Skills and experience: what you have learned how to do

- skills and experiences are things you have acquired; you can lose skills if you do not practice or use them
- you can continuously make additions to your skill base

Interests: what fascinates you, what you are drawn toward, what you are passionate about

- they are what makes "work" fun, why you look forward to it each day
- they should come from you–not from what pleases others

Personal style: How you interact with other people

- how you get energy–from contact and interaction with others or from being alone
- more satisfied working as part of a team or working autonomously

Family of origin: where you get your first ideas about "work"

- this is where you learn the importance placed on "work"
- you also learn where "work" fits into family's priorities

Values: what you hold most dear in life, why you do what you do

- can change throughout adult development

- what you do all day should have a relationship to your deeply held values

Goals: internalized drives that make all of us go

- successful people know where they want to go, what they want to be and what they want to accomplish

- goals point you in the right direction and help you get there

Through my own company, Career Launch International (www.careerlaunchint.com), I specialize in assisting students, recent graduates and 20-somethings discover their "best fit" educational and career options. Unfortunately it is beyond the scope of this manual to offer any direction about abilities. Objective ability assessments take several hours to complete and cost hundreds of dollars. There are currently no free, credible online ability assessments. As a new graduate, you are possibly experiencing a negative cash flow. When your cash flow improves, I suggest you consider making the investment in an ability assessment. It will serve you well.

> *You can't have everything you want, but you*
> *can have the things that really matter to*
> *you. ~ Marissa Mayer*

The next two exercises are online assessments. I am generally very suspicious of free online assessments for a number of reasons, including reliability, validity and confidentiality. The ones I suggest are from reputable organizations.

Assessments can often provide detailed information and insights in a short period of time. Remember to see this "detailed information" as possible clues.

Trying to interpret assessments by yourself is not advisable. Instead, you should share your results with someone you trust. Ideally this would be someone trained in interpreting assessments, possibly a career center counselor from your alma mater. They might also be able to offer other assessments and exercises.

All assessments suggested in this manual are provided for educational purposes only. They are not professionally administered. Therefore the results are not suitable for basing important decisions on; they can, however provide clues to help get you started.

Exercise #3: VIA Character Strengths Assessment

The first assessment comes from the field of Positive Psychology. Positive Psychology is the scientific study of strengths, well-being, and optimal human functioning. The field is founded on the belief that people want to lead meaningful and fulfilling lives, to cultivate what is best within themselves, and to enhance their experience of love, work and play.

The VIA Character Strengths Assessment comprises 24 character strengths and virtues, grouped into six core categories. These virtues are morally and universally valued, and they produce positive effects when we express them.

Via Classification of Character Strengths and Virtues (©Copyright 2004-2016, VIA Institute on Character. All rights reserved. Used with permission. www.viacharacter.org.)

1. ***Wisdom and knowledge:*** cognitive strengths that involve the acquisition and use of knowledge

    - creativity
    - curiosity
    - judgment
    - love of learning
    - perspective

2. ***Courage:*** emotional strengths that involve the exercise of will to accomplish goals in the face of opposition, whether that opposition is external or internal

    - bravery
    - perseverance

- honesty
- zest

3. *Humanity:* interpersonal strengths that involve tending and befriending others

    - love
    - kindness
    - social intelligence

4. *Justice:* civic strengths that underlie healthy community life

    - teamwork
    - fairness
    - leadership

5. *Temperance:* strengths that protect against excesses

    - forgiveness
    - humility
    - prudence
    - self-regulation

6. *Transcendence:* strengths that forge connections to the larger universe and provide meaning

    - appreciation of beauty and excellence
    - gratitude
    - hope
    - humor
    - spirituality

To complete the assessment, go to www.viacharacter.org.

Click on the gold button in the middle of the page: "Take the Free Via Survey."

> Using the worksheet provided in Appendix I and on www.fromeducatedtoemployed.com/the-forms/, list your top 5 strengths, and provide 2 examples of how and where you have used each strength.

If you found this assessment useful, you might want to explore more Positive Psychology assessments. You'll find several of these at www.authentichappiness.sas.upenn.edu.

Exercise #4: O'Net Assessment

This assessment focuses on **interests,** and was developed under the sponsorship of the Department of Labor and Training. It comes from O'Net, America's primary source of occupational information. This site has a tremendous amount of valuable career-related information.

John Holland's Vocational theory, often referred to as the "Holland's Codes," is used in O'Net's "interest" section. The central premise of Holland's theory is based on the idea that people choose jobs/careers where they can be around people like themselves.

According to his theory, most people in our culture fit into one of six personality types: **R**ealistic, **I**nvestigative, **A**rtistic, **S**ocial, **E**nterprising and **C**onventional (RIASEC). Holland concedes that it's nonsense to assume there are only six kinds of people in the world.

The assessment is composed of 60 items and measures six types of occupational interest. The following is a brief explanation of the six types:

1. **Realistic:** Realistic occupations frequently involve work activities that include practical, hands-on problem and solutions. They often deal with plants, animals, and real world materials like wood, tools and machinery. Many of the occupations require working outside, and do not involve a lot of paperwork or screen time or working closely with others. They are characterized as practical, straight forward/frank,

mechanical inclined, stable, concrete, reserved, self-controlled, independent, ambitious and systematic.

Realistic people are usually assertive and competitive, and are interested in activities requiring motor coordination, skill and strength. They like concrete approaches to problem solving, rather than abstract theory. They like to work with *things*. They value material rewards for tangible accomplishments.

2. **Investigative:** Investigative occupations frequently involve working with ideas, and require an extensive amount of thinking. These occupations involve observing, learning, investigating, analyzing, researching, evaluating and problem solving.

   Investigative people like to think and observe rather than act, to organize and understand information rather than to persuade. They tend to prefer individual- rather than group-oriented activities. They like to work with *data*. They value the development or acquisition of knowledge.

3. **Artistic:** These occupations frequently involve working with forms, designs and patterns. People in these occupations like to work in unstructured situations, using their imagination or originality. They like to attend concerts and art exhibitions. They are comfortable expressing themselves creatively. Artistic is characterized as creative, imaginative, unconventional, emotional, independent, and expressive.

   Artistic people do not like structure and rules. They like tasks involving people and are more likely to express their emotions than others. They like to work with *ideas* and *things*. They value creative expression of ideas, emotions and sentiment.

4. **Social:** These occupations frequently involve working with, communicating with, and teaching people. Individuals in these occupations like to inform, enlighten, teach, train and develop. They like to work in groups, do volunteer work and serve others. These compassionate helpers are skilled with

words. They are often described as cooperative, supportive, insightful, outgoing, friendly, and trustworthy.

Social people are different than R and I types because they are drawn to seek close relationships with other people and are less apt to want to be intellectual or physical. They like to work with *people*. They value fostering the welfare of others.

5. **Enterprising:** These occupations frequently involve starting up and carrying out projects. They sometimes require risk taking and often deal with business. People in these occupations like to direct, influence, lead, and manage others for organizational goals or economic gain. They are characterized as self-confident, assertive, energetic, adventurous, popular, ambitious, agreeable, extroverted, spontaneous and optimistic.

Enterprising people are good talkers, and use this skill to lead or persuade others. They value reputation, power, money, and status and will go after it. They like to work with *people* and *data*.

6. **Conventional:** These occupations frequently involve following set procedures and routines. People in these occupations like to work with data, have clerical or numerical ability, like structure, like carrying things out in detail or following through on other's instructions. They may enjoy working at a desk. They dislike unstructured or unclear work and interpersonal situations. They like to work with *data*.

Conventional people value material or financial accomplishments and power in social, political or business arenas.

Let's get started.

Go to www.mynextmove.org/explore/ip.

To start, click on the "Next" button at the bottom right side on the O'Net Interest Profiler box.

Remember: This is not a test.

Upon completion, you will receive your RIASEC score.

By taking the letters from your three highest scores, starting with the highest score first, then descending down to the next two, you have your Holland score.

For instance, let's say someone had the following scores: Realistic 16, Investigative 25, Artistic 9, Social 35, Enterprising 25 and Conventional 5. So their code could be SIE or SEI because Investigative and Enterprising both have a score of 25.

Next put "SIE Holland Code" in a search engine. This will generate different sites which give examples of careers which match this particular Holland Code. Just keep asking yourself what it is about those positions that interest you.

Use the worksheet, O'Net Interest Summary, provided in Appendix II and at www.fromeducatedtoemployed.com/the-forms/. The answers will provide some more clues about yourself.

Exercise #5: DiSC Assessment

Another popular assessment is the DiSC profile. It centers on four behavioral traits, which are identified as **D**ominance, **I**nfluence, **S**teadiness, and **C**onscientiousness. As an assessment, it is blind to gender, race, and age. The profile takes into consideration the unique ways that the four DiSC traits work together to influence personality and behavior. It identifies patterns of behavior, and can be used to implement solutions for maximizing an individual's strengths and minimizing weaknesses. As such, this is not a personality assessment, but rather an assessment of behavior in given circumstances.

Everyone is a blend of all four traits. However, there is usually one trait which is more prevalent. The four personality traits are defined as:

<u>D</u>ominant: Individuals with this trait place an emphasis on impacting the environment by overcoming opposition and challenges. They are motivated by winning, power, authority, competition and success. They can be described as direct, demanding, forceful, strong willed, driven, and determined, fast-paced and self-confident. They may be limited by lack of concern for others, impatience and open skepticism.

Influence: Individuals strong in this trait place an emphasis on shaping the environment by influencing or persuading others. They are motivated by social recognition, group activities and relationships. They are usually described as convincing, magnetic, enthusiastic, friendly, outgoing and optimistic. Sometimes they can be impulsiveness, disorganized and lacking follow through.

Steadiness: Individuals with this as their predominant trait place an emphasis on cooperating with others within existing circumstances to accomplish tasks. They are motivated stability, cooperation and providing support. They are best described as calm, patient, predictable, team players and stable They may sometimes be indecisive and have a tendency to avoid change.

Conscientiousness: Individuals strong in this trait value working conscientiously working within circumstances to ensure quality and accuracy. Clear performance expectations, opportunities to gain knowledge and quality work are motivating for individuals with a high Cs. They are usually described as logical, systematic, diplomatic and perfectionist. They may sometimes be overcritical and over analytical.

If you would like to find out more about yourself from this perspective, several free sites offer the DiSC. I suggest you consider the one offered by the Tony Robbins organization.

Exercise #6: Personal Attributes

A personal attribute is how people experience and describe you. To become aware of your attributes, you need to understand how people describe you. The following is a partial list of personal/brand attributes. This list is also available in Appendix III and at www.fromeducatedtoemployed.com/the-forms/.

Accepting Accountable Adaptable Adventurous Agreeable Altruistic Ambitious Amiable Analytical Approachable Articulate Artistic Aspiring Assertive Attentive Authentic

Balanced Believable Bold Brave Bright Brilliant

Calm Candid Carefree Caring Candid Challenging Charismatic Charitable Cheerful Circumspect Clever Compassionate Collaborative Committed Competent Communicative Compassionate Competitive Confident Concise Confident Considerate Conscientious Consistent Constructive Contemplative Cooperative Coordinated Curious Courteous Creative

Decisive Dedicated Dependable Detailed Determined Devoted Diligent Direct Disciplined Driven Dynamic

Eager Effective Efficient Eloquent Empathetic Empowered Encouraging Energetic Engaging Enterprising Entertaining Entrepreneurial Enthusiastic Excited Experienced Experimental Expressive

Fair Flexible Focused Free-thinker Friendly Fun

Generous Genius Generous Gentle Genuine Gifted Giving Goal-oriented Graceful Gracious Gregarious

Happy Hardworking Healthy Helpful Honest Hopeful Humble Humorous Idealistic Imaginative

Independent Industrious Influential Informative Innovative Inquisitive Intriguing Introspective Insightful Inspiring Intense Intuitive Involved

Just Kind Knowledgeable

Leader Lively Logical Loving Loyal

Mature Methodical Meticulous Mindful Moderate Moral Motivated

Natural Neat Nice Nurturing

Obsessive Objective Observant Open-minded Opinionated Optimistic Orderly Organized Original Outgoing

Passionate Patient Peaceful Perceptive Persistent Personable Persuasive Polite Positive Practical Pragmatic Precise Present Proactive Productive Professional Punctual Quirky

Rational Realistic Receptive Reflective Relaxed Reliable Respectful Responsible Resourceful Results-oriented Risk-taker

Self-aware Self-motivated Sensible Serious Shrewd Sincere Smart Straight-forward Strategic Studious Successful Sympathetic Systematic

Teacher Tenacious Thorough Tolerant Transparent Trustworthy

Unconventional Understanding Unique Unselfish Unusual

Valuable Venturesome Visionary

Work-oriented Wise Witty

Use the worksheet **Attribute Summary List,** Appendix IV and at www.fromeducatedtoemployed.com/the-forms/, to identify six attributes which describe you.

This exercise will help you answer variations of the following two questions typically asked in an interview:

1. How do you think other people would describe you? Please give 2 examples of each descriptor.

2. How would you describe yourself?

Exercise #7: Transferable Skills

A skill is a proficiency that is acquired by training and/or experience. You have been acquiring skills all your life, such as hobbies, sports, and part-time jobs.

Learning to ride a bike is a good example. At first, you needed training wheels or the firm hand of a parent to keep your balance. Steering, pedaling, keeping your balance and watching where you were going took all your attention. With enough practice, you could pedal alongside a friend and not even think about balancing, pedaling or steering.

Remember the first time you sent a text? Now it's second nature.

Skills can be broadly divided into two broad categories. The first group is referred to as *location specific*. You learn a skill in particular environment, but it has no application in any other environment. For instance, operating a locomotive is a very environment-specific skill.

The second is referred to as *transferable*. This means you can learn a skill in one environment and transfer it to another environment. These are skills that you acquired during an activity in your life. For example, you might have learned to be a team player from playing sports and working on class projects. This team-player skill can be transferred to the workplace. Other examples of transferable skills include communication (written and verbal) skills acquired during your academic years which can be transferred to your career.

Often the subject matter you studied in school is irrelevant to the type of career path you want to pursue. Transferable skills are the bridge between your education and your career path. They are a common language. Your transferable skills increase your marketability and support you as you transition from student to employee.

Your transferable skills are a way of telling a potential employer you have already done the work they described in the position description.

11 Transferable Skills Employers Require

The following 11 transferable skills are what employers commonly identify as being required in an employee. It makes sense that you need to be prepared to speak about them.

On the worksheet **11 Transferable Skills Employers Require**, from Appendix V and on www.fromeducatedtoemployed.com/the-forms/, identify examples of when you used the eleven transferable skills.

1. *Communication skills*
   - verbal

- written
- listening
- non-verbal (body language)

2. *Honesty/integrity*
3. *Team player*
4. *Initiative*
5. *Adaptability*
6. *Problem solving* (reasoning and creativity)
7. *Interpersonal* (getting along with others while getting the job done)
8. *Strong work ethic*
9. *Organizational/planning*
10. *Stress management*
11. *Computer* (email etiquette, spreadsheets)

Common Transferable Skills

The following is a list of common transferable skills. You might quite possibly have some skills that are not on this list.

Often by using synonyms you can widening your skill base without having to develop new skills.

Communication skills group

Articulating Describing Editing Explaining Expressing Facilitating Interviewing Interpreting Listening Negotiating Perceiving Persuading Proofreading Promoting Providing feedback Publicizing Reporting Selling Speaking Summarizing Telling Translating Understanding Verbalizing Writing

Creative skills group

Acting Brain-storming Composing Conceptualizing Conducting Creating Designing Detailing Developing Displaying Dramatizing Expressing Envisioning Generating Illustrating

Imagining Improving Inventing Modeling Organizing Painting Performing Photographing Printing Rendering Shaping Singing Sketching Symbolizing Writing

Human relations (helping and teaching) skills group
Advising Conflict Resolution Coping Consulting Counseling Empathizing Giving Helping Intervening Interviewing Instructing Mediating Mentoring Motivating Offering Reconcile Referring Rehabilitation Resolving Serving Sharing Supporting Tactfulness Teaching Tending Tutoring

Managing skills group
Auditing Budgeting Calculating Consolidating Controlling Deciding Delegating Determining Enforcing Evaluating Financing Implementing Integrating Monitoring Purchasing Recommending Recruiting Scheduling Supervising Troubleshooting

Leadership skills group
Advising Coaching Convincing Demonstrating Encouraging Engaging Guiding Influencing Inspiring Installing Leading Persuading Presenting Promoting Negotiating Team-building

Organizational/work skills group:
Administering Arranging Classifying Collecting Computing Defining Enforcing Estimating Filing Gathering Goal Setting Inventorying Monitoring Organizing Preparing Recording Retrieving Scheduling Self-directed Selecting Sorting Summarizing Supplying Systematizing

Researching/quantifying skills group:
Analyzing Charting Conceptualizing Diagnosing Detecting Discovering Disproving Evaluating Examining Experimenting Extracting Forecasting Formulating Gathering Hypothesizing Identifying Interpreting Inspecting Investigating Questioning Observing Predicting Prioritizing Problem-solving Researching Resourcing Studying Synergizing Synthesizing Weighing

Technical skills group:
Assembling Assessing Building Computing Constructing Designing Extracting Fabricating Fixing Installing Maintaining

Making Manufacturing Operating Producing Programming Repairing Setting-up Upgrading

The ***Common Transferable Skill Exercise*** worksheet, available in Appendix VI and on www.fromeducatedtoemployed.com/the-forms/, will help you identify your strongest skills

Putting it Together

You have discovered a lot of information about yourself. Making sense of it will take time. Here are some pointers to keep in mind:

- Things will come into focus more once you have engaged in The Graduate Advantage.

- Discuss what you have discovered about yourself with trusted friends, family members, your family's spiritual advisor or a school career counselor.

- Use other methods and exercises to broaden your understanding.

- Trust your intuition to help you make sense of the information you're gathering.

- You have been discovering some possible clues about who you are, and what is truly important to you.

- Learning about yourself is a lifelong journey.

Find out what you like doing, and get
someone to pay you for doing it.
~ Katharine Whitehorn

If you want to live a happy life, tie it to a goal, not to people or things. ~ Albert Einstein

SECTION 3:
Preparation
~ Laying the Foundation

Questions to Consider

1. Are you following your resume in or is your resume following you in?
2. Why is managing your inner world so important?
3. Should your resume be identical to your LinkedIn profile?

You spent years preparing to graduate. Doesn't it make sense you spend time preparing to launch your career?

This section encompasses a wide range of topics from branding to self-management. By the end of this section, you'll be ready to step into the action part of launching your career.

A solid foundation is essential to supporting a strong structure. This is no different than launching your career. If you choose to not invest the time and effort in the beginning, your results will reflect it.

The advertising slogan *You don't get a second chance to make a first impression* sums up the importance of thorough preparation. Everything from a poorly written LinkedIn profile to sloppy personal presentations at networking events kills your chances of building relationships. You will never know how many terrific opportunities you missed. But why risk missing any? Launching your career in this hyper-competitive job market requires professional preparation.

This means getting it right the first time.

Branding

Preparation is about building your brand. As a career launcher, your personal brand is defined as how potential employers experience you. Your personal brand encompasses your wardrobe, your grooming, your social media presence (LinkedIn, Facebook, etc.), and how you present yourself on your resume and related documents.

Personal branding is unavoidable. A personal brand is about choices. Being aware of your choices is the first step in the branding process. Personal brands are about self-awareness and being authentic.

It may surprise you to know that many hiring decisions are made on the basis of likeability. In some cases the likeability factor has overridden objective qualifications. This makes sense. Who wants to work with the "most qualified person" if you and your staff cannot get along with that individual? It can make for some pretty long days.

LinkedIn Profile

LinkedIn is a powerful tool in presenting your brand. Your profile is sometimes a person's first experience of your brand. What they see and read in a few seconds often determines whether they check you out further. The stakes are incredibly high.

LinkedIn is a social networking website designed for business professionals. It currently has over 480 million members in over 200 countries. Like Facebook, LinkedIn allows you to create a custom profile. Profiles on LinkedIn highlight education and past work experience, which makes it somewhat similar to a resume.

LinkedIn profiles are focused on your professional life, whereas Facebook and other social networking sites are focused on your personal life. *It's best to keep your personal and professional lives separate.* In other words, sharing personal information on your LinkedIn profile could damage your carefully crafted brand.

Nothing says "unprofessional" louder than sharing personal information on your LinkedIn profile.

The following is a generic LinkedIn profile format. Time spent searching "sample student LinkedIn profiles" online can provide additional ideas.

LinkedIn profiles are not usually written in a day. They usually take a week or so to put the final product together.

The usual process for creating a profile consists of researching, rough draft, feedback and final proof.

A LinkedIn profile consists of the following components:

- *Profile header* (your photo, headline, address, and industry you hope to be in)
- *Public profile URL*
- *Contact information* (websites, Twitter, email, phone, and address)
- *Summary* (professional experience, accomplishments and goals)
- *Education* (completed and still in progress)
- *Experience* (work/employment history)
- *Volunteer experience and causes*
- *Skills* (particularly ones which are aligned with potential employers)
- *Organizations*
- *Projects*

- *Honors and awards*
- *Courses*
- *Test scores*

Let's look at each component in more detail.

Profile header: Your brand in a nanosecond.

Your photo: The first thing people look at is your photo. If there is no photo, chances of the rest of your profile being read are usually slim. Your photo must present a professional image. The photo is the introduction to your brand.

People look at your photo before they decide to read further. The saying *A picture is worth a thousand words* sums up the value of your LinkedIn photo. Your photo helps people connect. According to LinkedIn, profiles with photos are 14 times more likely to be viewed by others. *Your LinkedIn photo is critical to making that personal connection with the reader.*

You can see how an unprofessional photo can destroy your chances of getting any Graduate Advantage opportunities.

Hiring managers have told me if a graduate can't get the first impression right, what does that say about them? What it says is they won't be invited to many interviews, never mind have hopes of landing Graduate Advantage opportunities.

A LinkedIn photo is what is referred to as a head shot. It's a picture of your face and the top of your shoulders. Your photo on your passport and driver's license are head shots. However, that's where the similarity ends.

Smile — it's your future.

There are three ways to obtain your head shot.

1. The highly recommended way is go to a professional photographer. They have the experience, lighting and know-how. Considering what is riding on creating your first professional impression, the money spent will be worth it.

2. Clip your photo from an existing picture and up load it. This is probably the quickest route; however, there are several major risks. These include poor quality, poor lighting, inappropriate background and dated attire. These pics are often referred to as a blast from the past.

3. Do-it-yourself. This one fits into a limited-cash-flow lifestyle. No, I'm not talking about a selfie. Even if you consider yourself the resident guru of selfies, get some else to take your picture. The following points can be used as a guide:

   - Using a smart phone or digital camera, it's possible to take a number of pictures from different angles and facial expressions. Then ask friends, family members and their friends which pic best represents you as a young professional.

   - Use natural light whenever possible.

   - Remember to smile. Breathe, and focus on feelings of confidence.

   - Look into the camera lens.

   - There should be no objects or pictures in the background. This will ensure the focus is on your face and shoulders.

   - Use background light to provide depth.

   - Follow the rule of thirds. The eyes should be one third of the way down from the top of the photo and off the one side.

   - Your attire, hair and for women, make up, should reflect the professional/brand image you want to project. Generally, conservative business-casual works well.

   - Explore different angles. Photos from above often provide the most favorable angles.

- Check with LinkedIn Help Center to ensure compliance with technical specifications for uploading your profile picture.

Headline: This is the career biographical information which is next to your profile picture. It gives people a short, memorable way to understand who you are as a professional.

This is your brand, tagline, micro-summary.

You have 120 characters to write a concise, memorable professional headline. A tagline can be a simple three-to-four-word phrase that relates to who you are professionally. You want people to think that phrase when they hear your name.

LinkedIn automatically puts your current position as your profile headline. Change it. This is an opportunity to stand out.

Here are some examples:

- Anthropology major specializing in survey design, interested in social media market research.

- PSU '16 Grad. Looking for sales or marketing entry-level position with global player.

Avoid common, overused buzzwords like *motivated, achieved, goal-oriented* and *social-media guru*.

You will need to put down a city and state or province as well as industry. If you don't know, put down a location where there are a lot of jobs that might interest you.

As for industry, this can be a toughie. If you aren't sure, that is okay as you can always change it later. Either way, you have to at least temporarily put down an industry that you might be interested in pursuing as a career.

Under the profile header, information from other sections will be used to populate the following:

- Current position
- Previous employers

- Education
- Connections
- Status update

Public profile URL: If possible, use your name. If you have a common name, this might not work. Try adding your middle initial if you have a common name.

When you sign up, LinkedIn automatically assigns you a group of numbers. Click on "edit" next to the URL and insert your new address.

Contact information: Only city, state/province. You can also add your Twitter and email addresses. If they don't support your professional image, don't use them. Using IM is not recommended.

Summary: This is where you speak about your experience and goals. This is a great opportunity to integrate keywords into your profile.

Your summary can be either written in the first- or third-person format. Third-person tends to convey an objective professional tone, whereas the first-person format makes it easier for the reader to emotionally connect with you.

You can use up to 2,000 characters. If you can use all 2,000 characters or close to that, great. But don't just use them to just fill white space. Actually, white space is an effective visual aid.

Remember, this is about speaking your brand. Readers lose interest very quickly when they feel they are being misled or charmed with elaborate and insincere words.

There are two distinctly different summary formats. The formats are referred to as the *standard format* and the *story format*. Both can be effective. The story requires more work, but can create a real connection with the reader.

You might consider using a quote to start off.

The **standard format** is based on the answers to three questions.

I have provided sample answers:

Who are you?

Finally, I have fulfilled the first part of my dream career goal which is to prepare for a career in International Human Resource Management. I graduated from McGill with a degree majoring in Human Resource Management and a minor in organizational psychology. Many of my electives were modern languages.

What do you do?

While in school, I worked as a Human Resource Management volunteer in several non-profit organizations which help new immigrants integrate into our culture.

Why should I hire you?

By the time I graduated, other non-profit organizations were asking for my assistance. This speaks to my ability to effectively use my knowledge in a wide variety of situations.

The **story format:** We are all overloaded with information, particularly digital. It's coming at us 24 hours a day, non-stop. The story format takes the reader out of the "more information" mode and helps you connect with them on an emotional level. A story well told differentiates you from other career launchers. It helps define your uniqueness.

Good stories have some common characteristics. They:

- evoke the senses: visual, auditory, kinesthetic and olfactory;
- are written for a particular audience, in your case hiring managers;
- tell how a short coming or failure was a stepping stone to an important lesson, possibly making you a potentially better employee;
- are not long;
- are chronologically structured;

- demonstrate your humanness, not your achievements; and

- require time to write and rewrite to "get it right."

If there is an immediate need to set up your profile (which there usually is), use the standard summary format while continuing to work on your story format.

Education: This is one of the areas potential employers read, after experience. If you have taken more than the customary time to complete your degree, you might consider not putting in your attendance dates. This is not a mandatory field.

Experience: This includes part-time, summer, internship, volunteer, and full-time work. As well, this includes any experience which demonstrates your interest in possible career fields such as study experiences abroad.

The experiences are usually presented in chronological order, from the most recent to your last experience. Your LinkedIn experience section should mirror your resume experience section:

- Company name

- Title (use keywords when possible)

- Location

- Time period

- Description

Skills and expertise: You can list up to 50 skills. Just because you have the opportunity to list 50 doesn't mean you have to. There are several things you need to keep in mind.

- If you list a skill, it's possible during an interview you could be asked for examples of when you used that skill.

- Are the skills you are listing aligned to your career goals? If not, why are you listing them? To fill space?

Volunteer experiences and causes: Research indicates that people who volunteer are 27% more likely to be hired than people who do not. Volunteer experience is often considered as valuable as paid experience.

Endorsements: Your connections can endorse the skills you list on your profile. Supposedly, accumulating a high number of endorsements for a skill adds credibility to your profile. The true value of endorsements is questionable. Hiring managers are aware (as they are also on LinkedIn) that endorsements are easy to obtain and are often self-serving. One of your connections endorses you and you in turn endorse them.

Projects: This is your opportunity to demonstrate how your educational projects and research have connections to possible career options.

Honors and awards: Don't restrict these to just academic. Sports and non-academic, including volunteer honors and awards, demonstrate your ability to achieve and get along with people in different environments.

Organizations: These include on- and off-campus organizations, as well as sports teams.

Test Scores: If you excelled in subjects that are aligned to your career aspirations, list your scores. A GPA above 3.0 is usually worth noting.

Courses: List all courses related to possible career options, especially if they are known for being challenging.

Also list relevant workshops, seminars, and special training.

Your Best LinkedIn Friend

Remember, the **edit button** can be your best friend as you set up your profile. As you gain a better understanding of "best fit" career options, you will want to make modifications to your profile.

Other Social Media

Don't say you weren't warned!

Although you might not be thinking of using Facebook and other social media for career launch purposes, potential employers might be using them to learn about you.

In one study, researchers found approximately 70% of viable applicants never make it to the interview stage. Potential employers saw something on social media about the applicant that made them decide not to "pursue" the applicant any further.

Resume: To Follow or Lead?

In the career launch strategy, the resume follows you into the interview situation.

This is a new paradigm. In the traditional job search method, you follow your resume into an interview. Let me explain the difference.

Using the career launch strategy, you are already known to the interviewer before they read your resume. They already know about you (through a Graduate Advantage, a referral, or other networking activity), and have checked your social media presence.

They have heard good things about you. They have a good idea who you are without having read your resume and covering letter. In other words, you are known—and then your resume and covering letter shows up (sometimes with you). This is what is meant when we say "your resume follows you in."

In the old-fashioned job search method, the interviewer doesn't even know you exist until they receive your resume. In a span of time, measured in seconds, your resume and covering letter have to convince the interviewer it's worth taking a deeper look. At this point, your resume is competing with perhaps hundreds of others for a second look. Since the interviewer doesn't know you from Adam (or Alice), good luck.

You have left it up to your cover letter and resume to create a positive enough impression to motivate the interviewer to Google your name. This is not the position you want to be in. If you are lucky enough to be invited in for an interview, your resume is already there. In other words, you "followed your resume into the interview." You can see why this strategy has such a low success rate.

Helpful pointers

A search of the web can provide you with numerous examples of recent graduate resumes, as well as informative discussions about them. So the information below touches on important points from a career-launch perspective.

You are going to need two resumes, a paper version and a digital one. Both say the same thing. That is where the similarity ends.

The paper is the traditional, old-fashioned resume. These are visually appealing through the use of font choices, bold and italic type, and grades and colors of paper.

Digital resumes don't have any visual appeal. These resumes are designed to be searched in keyword-searchable databases (a.k.a. resume black holes). Ever wonder where all the spray-and-pray resumes go?

If you are asked to submit a resume through "regular channels," this usually means digital. In these situations, make sure you also submit a traditional resume via personal delivery or courier service.

Paper resumes are considered out of date. And that is why they are so **effective**. It's so unusual nowadays to receive a paper resume and covering letter, that it gets attention. In fact, some experts say a paper resume can make or break a bid for a job if everything else is equal.

White printer paper won't work for resumes and covering letters. It doesn't say "professional." Use the type of paper referred to as *24 lb* or ideally *32 lb*. The "lb" symbol refers to the thickness of the paper. The paper has a more substantial feel.

Color matters just as much as paper weight. You want the paper to stand out without being obvious. Off-white, beige and almond shades work well. However, if you are interested in the creative fields, louder colors might be your best option.

With quality paper, you will be able to see a watermark, typically a logo, when you hold a sheet up to the light.

The texture of the paper is also important. Consider using 100% cotton paper, which is sometimes referred to as resume paper. If a local office supply store doesn't carry this type of paper, you won't have a problem finding a supplier online.

Typical Resume Structure

- *Name and contact information:* This should include your name, mailing and professional email addresses, dedicated phone number, and LinkedIn URL.

- *Summary:* What can you do for the organization? This answers the question "Why should I read on?" The answer to this question could be the headline from your LinkedIn profile.

- *Education:* Start with the institution you graduated from and its location. On the next line: degree, major, month and year of graduation, and GPA (only if 3 or above).

  Next line: *Coursework,* which includes only those courses relevant to the type of employment sought.

  Final line: *Projects, honors, thesis.* (This should be included if relevant to career aspirations.)

- *Experience:* This includes full- and part-time, summer, internships, and volunteer positions. Start with the most recent and progress back to your first experience. On the first line, list the company and time period, and the month and year of start and finish. If you are still employed, use "to present" instead of finish date. On the second line, list primary responsibilities.

- *Military (if applicable):* On the first line: organization, position, and title. The next line: start and finish dates of service. Then division and location. The last line contains duties and responsibilities.

- *Licenses and certificates:* These can include teaching and training certificates, CPR, software/hardware accreditations, etc.

- *Activities:* List membership on campus clubs and committees, including positions held and for how long.

- *Interests (optional):* Include volunteer activities, sports and hobbies.

As a general rule, I'm not in favor of using professional resume-writing services. When you write your resume, you are taking ownership of it. It's harder doing it yourself, but the writing process is another opportunity to learn more about yourself. The resume is part of your brand. As a recent graduate with limited experience, your resume should usually be one page.

Cover Letter

The purpose of the letter is to interpret the facts presented on your resume as they relate to a given position. This reinforces your qualifications for a position. As with the previous topic (resumes), there are ample examples of cover letters on the web.

Mistakes to avoid

From my extensive experience reading cover letters, I have noticed some common mistakes made by novice cover-letter writers. These include:

- Writing more than one page. If seasoned executives can do it in one page, you can too.

- Spelling and grammatical errors. Having a degree doesn't make you immune from making them.

- Using a generic format. Impersonal, fill-in-the-blank types indicate inability to communicate.

- Being verbose. The reader will quickly lose interest and never bother to read your resume.

Helpful pointers

The following key points should be kept in mind when you are composing your cover letter:

- Use proper business letter format, as most examples on the internet will demonstrate.

- Write succinctly, or enlist the help of a friend or parent until you feel comfortable doing it.

- Because you are using the career launch method, someone is usually referring you – so make sure you reference them.

- Be sure to reference any pertinent information you may have gained through networking, including Graduate Advantage activities and research.

- Consider using bullets. They save space and get to the point.

- Write your draft in a word processor with the spelling and grammar checkers turned on. These tools can greatly reduce spelling and grammatical errors.

Often, interviewers will read the resume first and then, if still interested, read the cover letter. Therefore, don't assume you are going to get the reader's attention in your cover letter.

A well-written cover letter supports your resume. There is a strong connection between the two. So even if the resume is read first, your covering letter still needs to make sense. As a poorly written cover letter doesn't support your resume, there will be no connection. This is evident when the resume is read first and then the cover letter. The reader is left with an impression she is reading about two separate subjects which are not connected.

Before you submit your cover letter and resume, read them in reverse order. Does your communication seem connected? Often, having a third party read your documents in reverse order gives you an objective perspective.

Phone Number

A phone number dedicated to launching your career is a necessity. When the phone rings, you know it's important. This is another way of separating your personal and professional life. With a dedicated number, you'll be able to decide whether to answer it or let it go to voicemail. When you answer your phone, you need to sound professional and relaxed.

You can always answer your phone and explain it's an inconvenient time to talk. You can then offer to call them back. Unless you have a pen and paper to write their name, number and any other pertinent information down, don't answer the phone.

Helpful pointers

Don't answer just because it rings. The biggest challenge career-launchers have with phones is answering them whenever they are free to talk, without any consideration as to where they are. Phones easily pick up background noise. Don't answer until you are in a phone-friendly environment.

A phone-friendly environment is free from TV, children, crying babies, pets, doorbells, and ringing phones. This is a place where there is silence.

Make sure you have a pen and paper to write down pertinent information.

Your voice message

Creating a professional voice message is an important part of your brand. Some of the voice messages I've heard speak volumes about an individual's creativity, imagination and fun side. Unprofessional messages tell the caller that you are clearly not serious about launching your career.

The following are some pointers to keep in mind when composing and recording your voice message:

- Keep it simple and straightforward.

- Don't use over-worked phrases such as, "Your call is important to me."

- Write down what you are going to say.

- Rehearse saying your message until it sounds natural.

- Smile while recording your message.

Here is an example of a voice message:

Hi, you have reached _____. I'm not available to take your call.

Please leave your name, number and a brief message at the sound of the beep.

I'll get back to you as soon as possible.

Thank you.

When you are using a phone for professional activities, you will need to be hands-free. Consider purchasing a smartphone stabilizer, usually under $10. This props your phone up and frees your hands. Or you might want to consider a Bluetooth device. Simple tasks, like taking down directions to get to an interview, are much easier when you are not trying to hold a phone in one hand and take notes with the other.

The problem with smartphones is their battery can go low—and usually at the most inappropriate time. The best way to avoid this is to have a designated landline. From a hands-free perspective, consider purchasing a speakerphone.

If you habitually answer your phone without thinking, I recommend you turn your phone off until you are in a phone-friendly environment. Don't risk possibly losing a Graduate Advantage opportunity because your caller couldn't understand what you were saying over the background noise.

Email Address & Etiquette

You will also need a professional email address. Your current email addresses most probably reflect the more relaxed you, the student you. Your email address is part of your brand.

Register a combination of your first and last names. If you have a common name, try adding your middle initial. Sometimes, with the free web-based email services, you have to try various combinations.

Remember to add a signature line including your LinkedIn URL with your outgoing emails. Most email programs let you set up a template signature line at the bottom.

Helpful pointers

Up until now, your email correspondence has been informal. As you launch your career, you'll have to ensure it reflects your professional status. The following points can help guide your email communication:

- Pay attention to the subject line. See this as a topic heading which is short and to the point.

- Use professional salutations such as *HI* or *Hello*, and in very formal situations use *Dear*.

- Use a title and a last name: Ms. Armstrong, Dr. Blackstone.

- Avoid using acronyms.

- Use proper capitalization and punctuation.

- Limit your use of exclamation points.

- Put the sending email address in only after you have proofread the email several times.

Skype or Similar Services

Use of digital video in business is growing fast, particularly as it pertains to employment. This will prove to be a valuable tool for launching your career. You will be able to set up Graduate Advantage interviews with individuals across the country—in fact, around the world. This is the closest thing to face-to-face meetings.

More and more companies are using video interviewing as part of their interview process. Skype is by far the most popular service provider. However, the most important thing to keep in mind is what VoIP your interviewee/interviewer is using.

Helpful pointers

We will discuss the actual mechanics of digital interviewing in detail later in the manual. In terms of preparation, besides setting up a Skype account, you'll need to think about your physical environment. Please consider the following points:

- Identify one room as your video-interview room, ensuring it's relatively sound- and interruption-proof.

- Whether you are going to use a webcam, phone or camera, make sure the microphone is making your voice sound clear and professional. If you are not satisfied, consider a separate microphone.

- Experiment to find the best angle. Usually the camera should be at eye level. Little changes in facial position alter other people's perception of you.

- The right lighting at the right angle is key. Google "lighting techniques for video interviews."

- The background should only be a wall in a neutral color. Consider hanging a bed sheet or a large piece of fabric from the ceiling.

- Make sure your Skype username and profile are professional.

Business Cards

Business cards are an important part of your marketing strategy. They have been around for a long time, and are still very popular simply because they work. Handing someone a business card is more professional that trying to quickly write your contact information on a piece of paper or napkin.

The back of your business card can be used to write someone's contact information, if they don't offer you their card. Pulling out your phone to type in someone's contact information can be awkward.

Business cards often make up part of your first impression. They help promote your brand, and are part of your professional image. In business settings, when you offer your business card people usually reciprocate with theirs. In social and other settings, offering someone a business card increases the chances they will remember you.

Helpful pointers

The following are guidelines for creating your business card:

- Include
    - your full name, as it would appear on your LinkedIn profile;
    - only your city, state/province (not the rest of your address);
    - your email address; and
    - your LinkedIn profile URL.
- Keep it simple and professional.
- Use the same or similar color as your resume paper.
- Consider using a printing company, such as Vista Print, which offers you access to hundreds of designs.

You will be pleasantly surprised at how effective a piece of card stock only 3.5 by 5 inches can be in supporting your career-launch activities.

Attire

Your attire should reflect your move from student to up and coming professional. What to wear to an interview is easily solved by asking the person who is setting up the interview what is appropriate attire for the interview.

The adage *You never get a second chance to make a first impression* speaks to the importance of your attire and grooming. It plays an important non-verbal part in successfully transitioning from graduate to employee.

Your appearance is made up of two components, attire and grooming. They are strongly interrelated. One without the other just doesn't work.

Considering the importance of attire, finding the money for some professional-style clothing is highly recommended. Professional doesn't mean the latest in fashion trends. It means traditional, or classic, quality clothing. If the interviewer remembers you for your fashion statement, you better keep looking—unless you want to work in the fashion industry.

When you are planning to attend a networking event, check with the events coordinator to find out what most of the people usually wear. This saves you the risk of projecting the wrong image.

Helpful pointers

The following are some suggested attire and grooming guidelines, subject to asking about "appropriate attire" for the situation you plan to attend. From your networking and Graduate Advantage experience, you will discover what is acceptable and appropriate.

You might consider some of the suggested guidelines as over-dressing. Generally, it is better to be over-dressed than under-dressed. It's hard to look "over professional."

Very seldom will you be criticized for dressing too conservatively. However, dressing too casually or informally can cost you the opportunity to build professional relationships, because you won't be taken seriously.

For Women
  Attire
  - simple suit with a skirt or pants
    - navy, black or dark gray

- skirt long enough so you can sit down comfortably; knee-length is best
- conservative blouse in a complementary color
- minimal jewelry (one ring per hand) and hair accessories
- small, conservative watch
- conservative shoes (no open toe or back), polished; a basic pump is flattering and versatile
- pantyhose in a neutral color (bare legs are not considered a good option).

Grooming
- professional hairstyle (conservative)
- light make-up
- no perfume
- clean, manicured hands
- subtle or clear nail polish
- non-scented (or very lightly scented) deodorant.

Bring along a black padfolio.

For Men
Attire
- suit in a solid color—navy or dark gray
- dress shirt
  - oxford cloth
  - long-sleeved
  - color-coordinated with your suit
- conservative tie; without a tie, you'll project a "casual professional" image
- belt, color-coordinated with your shirt and suit
- dark, solid-colored socks (interviewers notice details)

- conservative shoes, black (or brown); shined
- watch (traditional-looking)
- only your wedding/commitment ring (and, in Canada, your engineering ring).

Grooming
- clean and manicured hands
- recent haircut
- trimmed beard
- no aftershave
- non-scented (or very lightly scented) deodorant.

Bring along a black padfolio.

Needless to say, showering or bathing before any event is a given. I have interviewed people who have just come from the gym or a sporting event. If they couldn't fit in a shower before they arrived for an interview, they were saying very loudly:

- The interview isn't important to them.
- They don't have any time management skills.

Your clothes should always be neat, cleaned and pressed. An iron is a good investment.

References and Background Checks

If an organization is interested in you, they will ask for your references. References are individuals who can validate what you have told the interviewer about yourself. These are usually people in positions of authority who know you.

References can be divided into personal and professional.

Personal are usually friends, friends of your parents, religious and volunteer leaders, and other individuals who can speak about your character.

Professional references are former employers, colleagues, clients and professionals who can speak about your employability and work-related qualities.

Chances are you, as a recent graduate, are short of professional references. Employers understand this. Therefore, you can use coaches, professors or other professionals who can vouch for your skills and accomplishments. Research indicates that approximately 40% of all job applicants have supplied distorted or embellished information, or have omitted information on their application. This means potential employers take thorough reference checks seriously, and many employers are now using background checking organizations.

Background checks typically involve verifying past employment, educational credentials, credit history and criminal history (if any). These are sometimes done in conjunction with reference checks.

As a general rule, aim to have six professional references. Most organizations will only ask for three.

There are two reasons for six:

1. It gives you flexibility to choose the references who can best speak of certain skills you want to highlight.

2. If your first three can't be reached, you can offer another three.

When a potential employer wants to speak to a reference, they want to do it now. If an employer can't reach your references, they will usually park your application. The last thing you want is a job offer subject to reference checks, when your references can't be reached.

It's important to ask individuals if it's okay if you can use them as a reference. Explain you are about to embark on launching your career and you would appreciate their assistance.

If at all possible, ask these potential references in person. Assure them that before you submit their name you will give them a heads-up.

If you can't provide three professional references, you will have to offer some personal references. If this is the case, ensure the person to whom you are giving your references knows which references are personal and which ones are professional.

Never assume someone will be a reference. This is both inconsiderate and unprofessional. Being on the receiving end of unprepared reference inquiries, my responses were off the cuff.

Once you have consent from references, obtain the best phone numbers and emails to reach them. Ask them if there are times in the foreseeable future when they might not be available.

Letters of reference don't usually carry much weight even if they are on an organization's letterhead. A lot more information can be obtained from speaking with the person who wrote the letter. Reference checkers have a strong preference for having a conversation with a reference.

In terms of background checks, make sure your credit history is up to date. If you have been convicted of any criminal activity, check out the possibility of a pardon and be prepared to discuss this in the interview process.

Sometime it can take a while to track down potential references. Do it now. Don't wait until you are in the interview process. It might cost you a job offer.

Self-Management Tools

Sometimes the most difficult part of the career launch process is managing yourself. Getting off-track is easy. It's about staying focused, committed and positive. There are many ways to do this. The following are some of the most popular methods. The important thing is to find what works for you and commit to doing it regularly.

Setting Goals

Whatever methods you choose, goals need to be central to your self-management program.

A goal is a desired end result. Whether you realize it or not, you have been setting and achieving goals all your life. As a student, you had the goal of graduating (the end result) which you have achieved.

By learning to set and achieve goals, you are taking an important step in launching your career. As well, these lessons can be applied to other areas of your life.

> *Man is a goal-seeking animal. His life only*
> *has meaning if he is reaching and striving*
> *for his goals. ~ Aristotle*

Some of the benefits to incorporating goal-setting activities into your career-launch activities include:

- keeping you focused. It's easy to wander off and then wonder where the day/week/month went.

- improving your productivity. Goals help you become more organized.

- providing an objective self-accountability system.

- contributing to a sense of satisfaction. Research has shown that neuro-biologically the satisfaction of completing a task creates internal rocket fuel that energizes you to keep working toward larger goals.

- furnishing a structure. Goals provide a visual timeline which helps you plan.

The importance of goals is well illustrated by a Harvard study which took place between 1979 and 1989. The graduates of the MBA program were asked, "Have you set clear, written goals for your future and made plans to accomplish them?"

It turns out that only 3% of the graduates had written goals. Another 13% had goals, but they were not in writing. Fully 84% had no specific goals at all, aside from getting out of school and enjoying the summer.

Ten years later, the researchers interviewed members of those classes again. They found that the 13% who had goals that were not in writing were earning, on average, twice as much as the 84% of students who had no goals at all.

But most surprisingly, they found that the 3% of the graduates who had clear, written goals when they left Harvard were earning on the average ten times as much as the other 97% of graduates. *The only difference between the groups was the clarity of the goals they had for themselves when they graduated.*

A goal is a statement of a specific desired end result built on five criteria. **SMART** is the acronym for the five criteria:

- **Specific:** Goals should specify what needs to be accomplished—a description of a precise or specific behavior/outcome. Goals need to be concrete and use action verbs.

- **Measurable:** You should be able to measure whether you are meeting the goal or not.

- **Achievable:** The goal needs to be attainable within a reasonable amount of time. This criterion has to be within your control and influence. You must have the necessary skills.

- **Relevant** or **Reward:** The goal must have meaning for you. It is usually connected to larger goals and aligned to your overall life in general. What are you going to do or give yourself when you achieve the goal?

- **Time-bound:** This criterion identifies target dates, both a start and finish.

Here are some examples of career-launch goals:

Within 72 hours after establishing my LinkedIn profile today, I will have identified 20 LinkedIn members who are part of my alumni. When this is accomplished, I will go for a walk in my favorite park.

This goal is *specific:* identify LinkedIn members of your alumni. The goal is *measurable:* 20 LinkedIn members. This goal is *achiev-*

able because you have a LinkedIn profile, so finding other members is under your control. This goal is *relevant* because it supports your career-launch activities. Seventy-two hours meets the *time-bound* criterion.

Within the next 30 days, I will contact 10 people to set up face-to-face information interviews. When I accomplish this, I will buy myself a Cinnamon Swirl Latte.

This goal is *specific:* contact people to set up face-to-face informational interviews. "Ten people" meets the *measurable* criterion. This goal is *achievable* because it involves contacting people. Whether these people agree to a meeting is immaterial. This goal is certainly *relevant* because it supports your career launch activities. And it certainly meets the *time-bound* criterion, "within 30 days."

I will be employed by a manufacturing company in an entry level marketing position in this city within 90 days from today. When I accomplish this, I will do the happy dance.

This goal meets all the criteria but one. It doesn't meet the *achievable* criterion. The decision to hire you is outside your control. Let's rewrite it to include the achievable criterion:

I will professionally present myself to every manufacturing company's marketing department in this city within 90 days from today.

From my experience working with career launchers, the three most common reasons for individuals not reaching their goals are:

1. They aren't specific enough.
2. They don't have total control.
3. They don't want the goal badly enough.

The following goal cycle illustration is another way to understand the goal setting and achieving process.

Goal Cycle

Set Goal

Key Action

Measure Results

Evaluate Progress

Make Adjustments

Reach Goal

Celebrate

The more you celebrate, the better you feel about yourself and the more you want to accomplish

Stress Management tools

Transitioning to a career is perhaps the most stressful event in your life so far. Anything that breaks your routine causes stress.

Leaving your comfort zone is stressful.

Someone once said that launching your career is a mind game that is won or lost in your head. From my experience, I couldn't agree more with this perception.

There are many tools which can help you maintain your emotional equilibrium. The following three—mindfulness, visualization and anchoring—are offered as ones which could work for you. The important thing is to find ones which you are comfortable using and then utilize them regularly.

Never underestimate the value of regular exercise. Many stressed-out graduates have discovered the benefits of jogging and other forms of aerobic exercise.

Mindfulness

Mindfulness is one of the most popular versions of meditation. This technique centers around being aware of the present moment. Using this method, you leave behind any judging, thinking, or reflecting that may be part of your usual thinking patterns. You think of the moment as a breath of fresh air and focus on one breath after the other, moment by moment.

Following is a brief outline of the steps to practice mindfulness:

1. Sit in a comfortable chair or lie down in a comfortable position. Adjust your body until you feel relaxed. There should be no stress or tension on any given part of your body.

2. Think of this moment. Forget about anything in your past or future that you may have been thinking about and focus on now.

3. Hold this moment in awareness. Try, for as long as you can, to keep your focus on the moment.

4. Attend to your senses. Pay attention to what you smell, touch, hear and taste, as well as your breathing.

5. Focus on your breathing. Pay attention to your breathing without trying to change it. Feel the breath coming in and

out. Breathe gently in and out. Follow the air as it moves into your belly and then out again. If you want, you can close your eyes, but continue focusing on your breath. Keep feeling it going in and out.

6. Try to ignore your thoughts. Your thoughts naturally try to comment on your experience.

7. Anytime you notice that your mind is no longer focused on your breath, let your awareness recognize what's on your mind, and gently let it go.

8. Return to focusing on your breath, thus focusing on the present.

Practice for only a few moments to start with. At first, a few moments can seem like a long time. Be patient with yourself. As you become more comfortable with the practice, gradually increase the amount of time.

Choose a particular time each day to practice until it becomes part of your daily activities. It doesn't take long until you start noticing subtle shifts in your mood.

> *We become what we think about all day.*
> *~ Emerson*

Visualization

Visualization is a technique of using one's imagination to visualize specific behaviors or events occurring in one's life. This technique refers to the practice of seeking to affect the outer world by changing your thoughts and expectations—your inner world.

Visualization is similar to meditation, only it is more active and vivid. In visualization, you are encouraged to think actively about your goal. Visualization only works when you are calm, at ease and willing to give yourself time to focus. It is not a substitute for commitment and hard work.

This technique is frequently used by athletes to enhance their performance. It involves creating a detailed picture of what your goal would look like once it's accomplished. You visualize the goal over and over again with all your senses. (What do you see, what do you feel, what do you hear and what does it smell like?)

Oprah Winfrey, Anthony Robbins and Bill Gates have claimed visualization has played a significant role in their success. If it works for them, it'll probably work for you.

In your situation, you might want to practice confidently introducing yourself to business people or engaging in a Graduate Advantage. With enough time and practice, visualization can be an important tool in your self-management tool box.

> *To visualize is to see what is not there, what is not real—a dream. To visualize is, in fact, to make visual lies. Visual lies, however, have a way of coming true.*
> *~ Peter McWilliams*

Visualization is a skill. Like any other skill, it improves with practice. Here are some pointers for practicing visualization:

- There is no right or wrong way to visualize. Only through trial and error will you discover what works best for you.

- Visualization is best done alone and in an undisturbed environment.

- Being comfortable is important. A recliner chair works well.

- Start with something easy, such as what your next meal is going to look like, taste like, and smell like; what you will be wearing; how you will be feeling; what the room will look like; and what sounds you will hear.

- A critical key is emotional intensity. Really *feel* those feelings.

- Make sure you visualize in color, and don't be afraid to turn up the brightness in the color.

- Avoid visualizing on how you don't want things to turn out.

- Practice, practice, practice.

Anchoring

Anchoring is a fast way to access positive emotions on demand. It is an NLP (Neuro-Linguistic Programming) technique. It is easy to learn and has many applications. Anchors can be used before a Graduate Advantage or anytime you are stepping out of your comfort zone.

Anchoring is reminiscent of Pavlov's experiments with dogs. Pavlov sounded a bell as the animal was given food. The animals salivated when they saw the food. By presenting food and at the same time ringing the bell, they anchored the ringing to eating. So as soon as the dogs heard the bell they automatically started salivating.

Anchoring uses a stimulus. It may be a sound, an image, a touch, a smell or a taste used to trigger a consistent response.

When something is anchored, we react without thinking. For instance, you stop when you see a red light, a particular song reminds you of an old romance, or the smell of fresh-baked apple pie brings back memories of your grandmother. These are all anchoring experiences.

The advertising industry is a master at creating anchors.

Setting up an anchor

The following are the steps to set up an anchor:

1. Decide on the state you want to anchor. For instance, being confident.

2. Choose an anchor you wish to trigger the resourceful state. For instance, the thumb knuckle on your left hand being firmly rubbed by your index finger of your right hand.

3. Recall a memory when you felt super confident.

4. When you start feeling super confident, start rubbing your thumb knuckle with your index finger. This may take a couple of tries. You don't want to keep anchoring when the feeling is fading.

5. As soon as you reach the peak of the feeling of super confidence, stop rubbing your knuckle.

6. Now test it. Do something else for 30–45 seconds to change your attention. For instance, spell you name backwards.

7. For best results, repeat several times. This strengthens the anchor by establishing it at peak several times.

8. Think about how you might feel just before your first Graduate Advantage. Now fire your anchor. If you don't feel a difference, repeat the steps.

Either you are a star in your own movie, or you have a bit part in someone else's.

The Graduate Advantage

Questions to Consider

1. What makes Graduate Advantage opportunities so unique for recent graduates?

2. Is face time really worth getting ready for?

3. Can your life be changed in a mere seven seconds?

Graduate Advantage: What is it Exactly?

The Graduate Advantage is the core of the career-launch program. This is one of the key components that help you get ahead of hundreds of thousands of other recent graduates in this hyper-competitive job market.

Graduate Advantages are similar to informational interviews. For you they are truly your advantage.

Graduate Advantages are simply a short 15-minute meeting which you request with someone in a career field you are interested in learning more about. You are doing the interviewing. This short meeting provides you with some incredibly important benefits.

As mentioned in the introduction to this manual, you are in a unique position, as a recent graduate, to capitalize on the benefits of informational interviewing. That is why these interviews are called the Graduate Advantage. Nearly everyone has been in your situation, or they have seen family members and friends struggle to find their way. So when you reach out to people professionally, they are often willing to help you find a bridge from unemployed graduate to meaningful work.

The Graduate Advantage is the only super-bridge. It does have a toll: commitment and hard work.

Dangerous Assumption: Research indicates that, on average, 15 Graduate Advantages result in a job offer. Since there is a direct correlation between the number of Graduate Advantages and employment offers, it's natural to assume the quicker you do 15 Graduate Advantages, the sooner you will receive a career opportunity offer. This is a career-limiting assumption.

Keep in mind what the word "average" means. In this case, possibly after only two Graduate Advantages you'll receive an employment offer. On the other hand, you might have to do 50 before you see any results.

From my experience it's not the *number* of interviews which is the deciding factor but rather the *quality*. If you are prepared, learn from each Graduate Advantage, and improve, the numbers will be on your side.

Why Is the Graduate Advantage So Incredibly Important for You?

Discover best-fit career options

You now possess some knowledge about your interests, skills, values and strengths. Graduate Advantages help you find out where you have the best-fit options.

One way to figure out best-fit career options is to read books and do internet searches. Sometimes friends and family will offer their opinions.

It makes sense that the best way to find out what it's like to work in a particular field is to speak to people already doing work in your field of interest. They can share with you what an average day is really like. They can also share the challenges, pitfalls, and what it really takes to be successful in particular roles. You are getting the inside scoop. This is by far the quickest and most effective way to discover a possible fit. And it's free!

Practice your professional interview and presentation skills

There is nowhere else you are going to have the opportunity to sit in front of a manager and hone your interview skills. This is real life. Preparing for and conducting a Graduate Advantages is similar in many ways to an actual career launch interview. The only real differences are that you are asking the questions and the interview is short. Once you have conducted a number of successful Graduate Advantages, handling yourself professionally in a job interview will come easily.

Everything else about the two types of interviews is the same: preparation, research methods, appropriate attire, anchoring, non-verbal communications, etiquette, and post interview communications.

Practicing your interviewing skills by video recording will improve them. However, the Graduate Advantage can be seen as your personalized acceleration program.

Through the Graduate Advantage process, you become comfortable speaking with managers and professionals from many age groups and cultures.

Graduates often take a long time to find meaningful employment because there is so much to learn about effective career opportunity interviewing. Graduate Advantage opportunities are a critical incremental step in expanding your comfort zone boundaries.

Increase your self-confidence

Nothing increases your self-confidence more than completing a challenging task successfully. Self-confidence is the fuel which moves you beyond your comfort zone. It creates and reinforces the idea that what you focus on and work at, you accomplish. By successfully completing a number of Graduate Advantages, your self-confidence naturally grows. As your self-confidence grows, your goal of finding meaningful employment becomes more believable and real. You will surprise yourself with how self-confident you are in a career opportunity interview.

It's normal to experience many emotions as you transition from successful student to newbie employee. The single most important experience which will facilitate your successful transition is the Graduate Advantage.

Facing your doubts, pushing yourself and reaching your goal are the real lessons learned when you step out of your comfort zone through the Graduate Advantage. This is the perfect experience to facilitate these lessons. Once you have mastered the Graduate Advantage, career opportunity interviews won't seem like daunting tasks.

And once you have tasted the exhilarating feeling of living beyond your comfort zone, your career-launch activities (and in fact your life) become easier.

Start building professional relationships

Since an individual has offered to give you 15 minutes of their time, they have essentially agreed to help you. One of the biggest mistakes graduates can make is seeing the interview as just a 15-minute interaction. Start seeing the Graduate Advantage as the beginning of a professional relationship. This relationship could generate referrals to other Graduate Advantage opportunities or vacant positions in the invisible job market.

Connect to the invisible job market

As mentioned previously, approximately 80% of all position vacancies are on the invisible job market. The Graduate Advantage is by far the most effective method of accessing this market. Once you have completed a few Graduate Advantages you will start to become aware of vacant positions. Your professionalism and confidence will put you on the employment radar of your interview-ees and their referrals.

Invaluable preparation for job interviews

Graduate Advantage opportunities are your career launch train-ing wheels.

The information you gather from your Graduate Advantage expe-rience can be used to demonstrate why you are a good fit in career opportunity interviews. You can demonstrate this in two ways:

- Weave information obtained from the Graduate Advantage into your answers.

- Reference this information when you are asking questions.

Combining self-awareness with interview experience and first-hand career specific knowledge makes you an exceptional candi-date for any position you believe is a good fit.

Life shrinks or expands in proportion to one's courage. ~ Anais Nin

The First Impression

Your career-launch possibilities can dramatically change for better or for worse in seven seconds, often without you saying a word.

You never get a second chance to make a first impression.

Seven seconds is the average length of time you have to make a first impression, whether face-to-face, or via Skype. On the phone, you possibly have a bit longer time, and words play a role.

A popular interpersonal communication model says our commu-nication consists of physiology, tonality and words. According to this model, physiology—which consists of facial expressions, ges-tures, eye movements, body postures, grooming and attire—makes up 55% of what we say. Tonality—which refers to tone, intonation and volume—makes up 38%. And words are only 7%.

Because the first seconds are often non-verbal, the physiology component plays a larger role. An incredible amount of generally accurate information about you is picked up in just a few seconds.

Once a first impression has been made, it's difficult for you to change it. Although we are all familiar with the *metaphor never judge a book by the cover,* we do it all the time.

As humans we are "hard wired" to make very quick assessments. Our prehistoric ancestors had to make life-or-death decisions in seconds. Research has shown that it takes only one-tenth of a second for us to judge someone and make a first impression. Usually within 30 seconds, the first impression has been confirmed.

Psychologists have a term for this lightning-fast ability to assess people and situations. It is called "thin slicing." It describes the ability to find patterns in events based on "thin slices" or narrow windows of experience. This results in making very quick decisions with a minimal amount of information. Malcolm Gladwell wrote an excellent book on the subject, *Blink: The Power of Thinking Without Thinking.*

Research has shown that often after a few seconds, interviewers will attribute to a candidate such traits as friendliness, confidence, likability, trustworthiness, competence, or politeness, as well as nervousness, coldness or distance. Within moments, you can be seen as plastic and disinterested, or enthusiastic and warm.

Here is the really interesting part: *In most cases, interviewers can't explain how they arrived at these traits.* This is because thin slicing takes place at an unconscious level. The candidate (you) has encoded non-verbal mini-traits which the interviewer picks up and translates into attributes.

These mini-traits can include smiling or negative facial expressions; poor posture; fidgeting; making eye contact; or facing another direction.

You get the picture by now. As a career launcher, you must become a master of first impressions. This is about sinking or swimming.

Remember, if you are likable people are inclined to listen to you and, most importantly, remember you.

Most people usually use some parts of the non-verbal mini-traits on a hit-or-miss basis. The good news is practice, practice and more practice can improve your ability to deliver your critical first impressions. The first step to becoming a master is to become aware of what you are doing. The following are the key non-verbal mini-traits:

- **Posture:** If you are standing, imagine an invisible thread attached to your head and connected to the ceiling. The position of your back is the foundation of your body language. A straight but relaxed spine puts you in a mental and physical state from which words flow smoothly and easily.

- **Attitude:** It shows. Do an anchoring exercise.

- **Smile:** A smile says "I'm approachable and friendly." There is a difference between a fake smile, often referred to as a sales person's smile, and a genuine one. A fake smile appears abruptly, stays the same for a disproportionate amount of time, then quickly disappears.

  Genuine smiles emerge more slowly and gradually. They are brief but repetitive. Even a fleeting smile has the capacity to connect subconsciously with another person and set off a mini emotional high in that person.

  > *Your smile will give you a positive*
  > *countenance that will make people feel*
  > *comfortable around you. ~ Les Brown*

- **Eye Contact:** When approaching or being approached by a person, make eye contact. Eye contact is expected to be regular but without glaring. Looking at someone's eyes signals interest and openness.

- **Appearance:** This topic has been covered in the preparation section.

- **Handshakes:** As a recent graduate, you probably haven't had much practice handshaking. Always stand up to shake someone's hand. A firm handshake demonstrates confidence. Your hand should be dry and warm.

  Women with a firm handshake make a favorable impression. They are judged as confident and assertive.

  The basic handshake consists of these steps:

  1. Look into the other person's eyes and smile.
  2. Start your verbal introduction as you extend your hand.
  3. Extend your hand with your palm facing sideways.
  4. Ensure the web of your hand touches the web of the other person's and there is palm-to-palm contact.
  5. Pump your hand 2 to 3 times or 3 to 4 seconds.

It takes practice to get the right amount of grip. Both the "fish hand" and the "iron man's grip" need to be avoided.

Sometime within the seven-second timeframe, there might be an initial verbal exchange. At this point, your communication will shift to 55% body language, including attire; 38% how you speak (tonality); and 7% will be the actual words you speak.

For instance, in networking events you will approach a fellow networker and introduce yourself with confidence and enthusiasm. Say "Hi, my name is Beverly Higgins" while extending your right hand to start a handshake. Or a fellow networker will approach you and introduce him or herself.

Your response is, "It's a pleasure, Harry (or "It's great to meet you, Harry"); my name is Beverly Higgins." Through a combination of saying something positive, such as "It's a pleasure to meet you," and using the person's name, you have successfully connected with that person.

At the beginning of a Graduate Advantage or career opportunity interview, the conversation can go several different ways. As the interviewee or interviewer approaches saying your name, confidently stand up, extend your hand and smile.

They will usually say, "Mr. Higgins (or: Brian Higgins), my name is Debra Walsh." Your response can be, "It's a pleasure to meet you, Ms. Walsh." Or they may say something like, "Mr. Higgins, my name is Debra Walsh, how are you (or: Did you have any problems finding us)?" Your response should be something like, "Excellent, and yourself, Ms. Walsh; thank you for meeting with me today," or "No problem, thanks for meeting with me, Ms. Walsh."

You will notice in the networking scenario the person's first name was used. In the interview scenario, Ms. was used. As a general rule, it's better to be on the conservative side, regardless of whether they are in your age range or not. Most people will respond to a formal title (prefix/honorific) by requesting you use their first name.

Graduate Advantage: The 3-Step Process

The Graduate Advantage is divided into 3 steps: *preparation*, the *interview*, and the *post interview*.

Preparation

In the first step, preparation, you are getting ready. This involves researching the interviewee, their company and industry, then reviewing your questions. Choose your attire. Make sure your padfolio has paper, a functioning pen or pencil and your business cards. You will also need a watch.

Research

The following information needs to be researched:

- What industry does the company belong to?
- What does the company do?
- Who is the interviewee?

Why do you need to know what industry the company belongs to? Interviewees often expect you to have a basic understanding of their environment. This demonstrates you are interested. You have taken the time to learn about them. You're a professional.

Every company belongs to an industry. Non-profit and government agencies belong to sectors. An industry or sector is basically a group of businesses or agencies which provide similar products or services.

Because you are asking for information, there is not an expectation you will be an expert on the company or industry. By following the steps below you'll gain sufficient information:

- To learn about the industry a company belongs in, use Google. In the search box, describe what the company does (i.e. fast food, wood flooring manufacturing, e-learning) followed by the word "industry." This will provide you with a good overview.

- The information you need to learn about the particular company can be obtained using Google search, the company's website and their LinkedIn page.

You don't know how the interview will unfold. For instance, you might impress the interviewee. After the interview, they might decide to introduce you to one of their colleagues. At this point, the Graduate Advantage is over and an unofficial "real" interview has begun. This colleague might want to discuss the industry and the company in more depth. You need to be ready. The following example illustrates the value of being prepared.

At the end of Alisha's Graduate Advantage her interviewee casually asked, "What do you know about us?" Alisha had done her research. After her reply, the interviewee said, "Impressive," and asked if she had time to meet one of his colleagues.

No, she didn't get a job offer from the company. But what did happen was this colleague referred her to a colleague in another company who granted her a Graduate Advantage. This eventually led to a career opportunity interview which she converted into a job offer. Alisha claims that having knowledge about the company was the catalyst.

Equipment and attire

We covered attire in the previous section; if you skimmed past that part, please go back and take another look. That's where we introduced two items you may have wondered about: the padfolio and the watch. Both are necessary equipment.

- A padfolio provides paper to take notes on, and a place to put business cards and your interview questions. Having the questions written down, even in bullet form, relieves you of trying to remember them.

- A watch allows you to stick to your schedule. You can't use your phone to tell the time because you turned it off and put it away before the interview.

If your interview will be via Skype, check that your equipment is fully operational at least one day before the interview. Call a friend. If you have added a third-party recording app, you can review your call. Remember, practice looking into the lens, not the computer screen. Make sure you won't be interrupted and your work area is clear.

If your interview will be by phone, check to make sure your hands-free feature is operational.

Time

You have asked for 15 minutes of the interviewee's time. To demonstrate your professionalism, you must stick to that commitment. Once you are in the interview, make sure your watch is visible. (Remember, your phone is turned off.)

If you are meeting the interviewee, how long is it going to take you to get from your place to their office? You should plan to arrive 5 to 10 minutes before the agreed upon meeting time. Ideally, you should plan to arrive in the general geographical area 20 minutes before the interview. Aiming for 20 minutes helps compensate for any unexpected delays. If you are driving, know your parking options.

Interview questions

Your questions can be divided into three groups: company or industry, the fit, and closing. I recommend one question about the company or industry. Then move onto the interviewee questions. Generally having a total of seven questions is sufficient. Prepare three core or key questions, two "would be nice if answered" questions and two questions just as backup in case the first five questions are answered quickly. Make sure you leave time for the closing questions.

The following is a list of fairly typical questions. Please feel free to reframe them to reflect your interests and personal style. Choose the questions that "fit" your situation.

Industry

- What do you think draws people to this industry?
- Did the industry play a role in helping you decide on working for this company?

Organization

- How would you describe the corporate culture?
- What work related values are most important in this company?
- What personal attributes are most valued by the company?

Interviewee

- Can you describe a typical day?
- What are some typical goals and objectives of this position (or this type of position)?
- What part of the job do you wish you didn't have to do?
- What do you need to know to be successful in this job?
- What skills are critical in this type of position?

- What skills do you use the most?
- What experiences and education prepared you for this job?
- What kind of team activities do you participate in?
- What advice would you offer someone thinking of entering this field?
- What was the hardest thing you had to learn about doing this job?
- Did your initial expectations differ from actually doing the job?
- How did you get this job?
- How do most people get into this field?

Closing

- What trade associations and publications or journals should I know about?
- Who else would you recommend I speak with regarding this field?
- As I continue my research, I'm sure I'll have more questions. Would you mind if I stayed in touch?

Consider using all three closing questions. In fact, the third question is a must.

The Interview

The interview is the second step. This is the crux of the Graduate Advantage.

If the interviewee has a difficult name to pronounce, ensure you have the correct pronunciation.

If you haven't spoken for a while, do a few voice exercises.

Arrive 5 to 10 minutes before the meeting—ideally 5 minutes, but no more than 10 minutes.

Smile confidently. Tell the person who greets you, "I'm here to meet _____."

While seated, do an anchoring exercise. Check to make sure your phone is off. If there are no company magazines or company literature to leaf through, open your padfolio and review your questions.

Now, focus on your seven-second first impression opportunity. As the interviewee or a receptionist approaches and states your name, stand. As the person introduces him or herself and extends a hand, you reciprocate. Then follow the person into the office or meeting room. Wait until the interviewee sits down before you sit down.

If the interviewee does not engage in an icebreaker question or statement, consider this a green light to start your questions— unless there is some common bond which you want to touch on (for example you attended the same school, live in the same neighborhood, etc.)

Thank the interviewee for agreeing to meet you.

Briefly state that as a new graduate you are trying to figure out the best possible fits for your skills and interests. You have been told that the best way to learn about work in different fields is to speak with people in fields which you are interested in.

Ask if it's okay to take notes. These can be just a word or phrase summing up an idea. You don't want to slow the pace of the interview with note-taking. By the way, I haven't heard of anyone objecting to note-taking.

Always be aware of your non-verbal communication and adjust accordingly. Randomly acknowledge the interviewee's answers with head nods, smiles, and an occasional, "That's interesting" or "That's a good point."

Sometimes the interviewee will make a really interesting point. You would like to explore it further. At this point you have two options. The first is to divert from the prepared questions and pursue the interesting point. The second is to simply make a note and keep moving. If you have time at the end, you can address the interesting point. If you are a relative newbie to the Graduate Advantage, I suggest you make a note of it and keep moving. It's too easy to lose track of time and focus. On the other hand, if you are starting to feel like a pro, consider diverting to the new point.

Occasionally at the close of the interview you might be asked for a copy of your resume. You have two possible responses:

- If you have just started doing Graduate Advantages, you might say you are currently working on one, and would be happy to forward a copy when completed. You might ask something to the effect of, "What did I say in the meeting which piqued your interest?" If the interviewee identifies a particular position, ask if it would be possible to obtain a copy of the position description. (Position descriptions are discussed in Section 6.) These can be a wealth of information about the position, and will help you craft both your resume and covering letter.

- If you are farther along in the Graduate Advantage process, consider saying, "I don't have one with me but would be happy to forward a copy." Then ask for a copy of the position description.

The interviewee will probably want an electronic copy. Make sure you also deliver a paper copy of your resume and covering letter.

As a general rule, you never want to submit a resume without first finding out about the position.

The Post-Interview

This is the wrap up and paper work stage.

As soon as you get home, sit down and review the interview. If you wrote any one-word answers, expand on them. Before you forget any details, answer the following questions:

- Did I remember to do an anchoring exercise?

- Did I remember to focus on the 7-second first impression opportunity?

- Was I aware of my non-verbal communication throughout the interview?

- Which question generated the best answer?

- Which question(s) possibly need rephrasing?

- What was the most important thing I learned?

- How does the information I acquired today line up with my strengths, skills and interests?

- From what I learned today, what questions do I want to ask in my next interview?

- What could I have done better?

If you obtained the interview through a referral, now is the time to get back to that person. Write a brief thank-you email for the referral. You might want to mention how helpful the interviewee was in explaining your field of interest.

A thank-you email to the interviewee for sharing their time and knowledge is mandatory. If the interviewee has agreed for you to stay in touch, mention you will take the liberty of doing so.

Digital Interviews

You need to put the same time and effort into preparing for a digital Graduate Advantage as you would for a face-to-face interview.

Remember, the interviewee usually only sees your face from a few inches above the head to the top of your shoulders. Your face conveys all the non-verbal messages.

Establishing rapport can be more difficult in a digital interview. We are accustomed to seeing the whole person, not just a face on a screen. In a digital interview, 55% of your communication is impacted by how you use your face alone.

To help you remember to look into the lens, place a small picture of the interviewee on top of the lens. It's too easy to speak to the person's face on the screen.

Double check to ensure you have set up your room as discussed in the preparation section. Check to ensure you have closed other programs on your computer.

Ensure you have the correct pronunciation of the interviewee's name.

If you haven't spoken for a while, do a few voice exercises. Have a glass of water available if your voice sometimes loses its clarity.

Minor sounds like rustling papers or clicking pens add distracting noise. They can break the focus and flow of a conversation. Make sure you only have the interview questions, paper to write answers on, and at least two functioning pens or pencils in front of you.

Before you dial, sit up straight, shoulders back, holding your head straight. As soon as there is a connection, smile. A smile says, "I'm friendly and approachable." Show you are interested and engaged by leaning in slightly.

During the first seven seconds of a digital interview, you will do a digital handshake and exchange verbal greetings. A digital handshake is simply a slight shoulder bend, eyes forward, and a slow, confident, professional nod. Make your verbal greeting count. Express some form of thank-you, such as "Thank you for agreeing to speak with me today."

Since there can't be any exchange of business cards, make sure you have the interviewee's full contact information.

Be sure to follow the same post-interview process outlined for a face to face interview.

Phone Interviews

Phone interviews are by far the most difficult to conduct effectively. You don't have the luxury of non-verbal communications. Without body language clues to provide feedback, it's difficult to assess your effectiveness.

Prepare for this type of interview as you would for an in-person or digital, including attire. You feel professional when you dress professionally.

During a phone interview, 70% of how you are perceived is based on your tone of voice and only 30% on your words. This means it's not so much what you say as it's the way you say it that counts. You must actively listen to the interviewee and ensure your voice sounds enthusiastic and clear.

Ensure your environment is free of distracting and potential noise makers. This includes turning the ringer off any other phones you have in the room. If you are using a mobile phone, make sure the battery is fully charged and properly mounted on the hands-free unit.

As mentioned previously, if you haven't spoken for a while, do a few voice exercises. Have a glass of water available.

The secret to a successful phone interview, besides preparation and practice, is to smile. A simple unseen smile is picked up by the interviewee. In fact, consider putting a smiley face or a smile sign in a visible place when you are on the phone.

Make sure you follow the same post-interview process outlined for a face-to-face interview.

Final Thoughts

- For some reason, interviewee's answers are sometimes shorter than expected. Having a few extra questions might be a good idea.

- If doing in-person Graduate Advantages seems too far out of your comfort zone, start smaller. Aim first to do a few phone interviews. Once you have gained some confidence, consider doing some digital interviews. Then start face-to-face. It's critical to do in-person interviews. By mastering them, you will have built a solid foundation to successfully participate in a career opportunity interview.

- Let's face it: you are probably going to feel nervous, if not overwhelmed, by meeting professionals and asking them questions. Just remember that the people you are interviewing were once where you are now. You will find they are usually supportive and non-judgmental. By approaching a Graduate Advantage as a learning process, you are taking the pressure off yourself to get it right from the start.

Anything is possible if you've got enough nerve.
~ J. K. Rowling

SECTION 5:
Discovering Graduate Advantage Opportunities

Questions to Consider

1. Why are Graduate Advantage opportunities so important?

2. Do mini brand bites really work?

3. Can your life be changed in a mere seven seconds?

Networking

The usual way to discover Graduate Advantage opportunities is through networking.

When you hear the word "networking," you might conjure up images of a small convention room filled with people talking very fast to anyone who will listen. Unfortunately, this caricature has been perpetuated for too long.

Networking is about relationships building. It is never about asking for a job. Networking is a mindset, not an event.

For career-launching purposes, networking is about cultivating relationships with people who can connect you to Graduate Advantage sources. This in turn will connect you to the invisible job market.

As you move forward in your career, networking will continue to play an important role. Lasting professional relationships are built on reciprocity. At first people will help you. However, at some point you need to return the favors. Saying thank-you is important, but your reciprocal actions over the long run are critical.

Networking is a skill. Like any other skill, it is learned and improves with practice.

To be successful at networking, you need to see networking as something you do anywhere and everywhere within socially appropriate contexts. It has to be a way of life. As someone just out of school, face-to-face networking is going to take you out of your comfort zone, possibly in a big way.

Networking is about making connections. Connectors are anyone willing to help you launch your career. They may grant you a Graduate Advantage opportunity, or they may provide you with the name of someone you could speak to. They are all contributing to launching your career.

People often assume that their contacts are their Connectors. There is a big difference. A contact is anyone you know. This can include family members, friends or people you meet. Connectors are contacts who are willing to help you launch your career.

Networking can be done face to face, by Skype, by email or on the phone. Your first choice should always be in person, followed by Skype, phone, and lastly email.

At this point, your goal is to engage in Graduate Advantage opportunities. Don't worry about getting career-opportunity interviews. You need the opportunity to learn and practice your interview skills before moving into the invisible job market. What you will find is that the more Graduate Advantages you complete, the more visible the invisible job market becomes.

The following diagram illustrates the ways a potential relationship with a contact can go.

Connector Development Illustration

1) You ⟶ **Contact = Dead End**

2) You ⟶ **Contact** ⟶ **Connector A = Information**

3) Information ⟶ **Contact** ⟶ **Connector B =** | **Graduate Advantage Opportunity**

In path #1, you make a contact. This can range from meeting someone at a networking event to reaching out to an alumni through LinkedIn. For whatever reason, they can't assist you.

In path #2, you make a contact who provides you with some relevant information, which makes them a Connector (Connector A). This information leads to illustration #3: another contact who agrees to a Graduate Advantage opportunity (Connector B).

In reality, path #2 can have many connections before you obtain a Graduate Advantage opportunity. As well, at any given time you will have multiple Connector activities on the go.

Connectors In Person, Online or In Print

Face time verse screen time: *Face time* refers to face-to-face interactions. This can include anything from having a chat with a possible Connector in a fast-food line to conducting a Graduate Advantage on Skype. *Screen time* refers to using your computer for research, email, and other related activities.

Face time is more important than screen time. In fact, face time is critical to successful networking. Screen time has to be seen as supporting your face-to-face networking. If you spend more time in front of a screen, don't expect to launch your career in the near future.

Face time is about stepping out of your comfort zone. You only have so many hours per week to devote to launching your career, so make them count.

Your alumni connection

One of the best places to start building your online connections is your alumni through LinkedIn. Also, you might want to touch base with the alumni office at your school. They would know of chapters in your area. Remember, the primary purpose of the alumni office is to raise money.

Alumni were in your position at some point and appreciate the challenges you are facing. Approached professionally, they can become some of your best Connectors.

To get started, log into your LinkedIn account:

- Click on "My Network" (top bar).

- In the drop-down menu, click on "Find Alumni." You will find out about where they work, what they do and where they live.

- In terms of priorities, consider focusing on where they live first. Alumni members living close to you will provide the best opportunities for face-to-face meetings.

- Next, in the search box on the top of your home page enter "[your school] alumni groups." You can join whichever groups align with your career aspirations. Once you're a member, you are able to scan the groups for potential contacts in your area which can be converted to a connection.

Groups

There are over a million groups on LinkedIn. You are allowed to join up to 50. To stay focused, join only groups which align with your career interests. Consider limiting yourself to five to start.

It's too easy to fall into the trap of spending your time joining and participating in groups and avoiding face-to-face networking.

Groups are a great place to find out current issues and challenges in a particular field. After you have followed and possibly contributed to some conversations, you might consider posting your interest in learning more about a particular aspect of this field. Remember, you are trying to learn more about a particular subject, not ask for a job.

Facebook can play a limited role in sourcing possible contacts. Check to see if your local alumni have a page. Friends (and friends of friends) have the potential of becoming Connectors. By converting your social media contacts through face-to-face meetings, you will be able to grow your connector group.

When it's not possible to initiate a face-to-face meeting, consider using a VoIP like Skype. This is a real win-win for you. First, the person gets to experience you. Second, you learn more about a particular field. Third, you have an opportunity to practice your interview skills. Fourth, distance is no longer an issue in finding Connectors.

Professional and trade publications

These can be a treasure chest for making contact with potential Connectors. Nearly every profession and industry has at least one publication. These publications number into the thousands.

A publication covers a specific profession or industry. Its purpose is to deliver information about new developments, current events, issues and trends.

Every article in a publication is written by someone who is knowledgeable and often seen as an expert in a particular field. Approached professionally, authors can be a wealth of knowledge and possible connections.

There are two avenues to finding these publications:

- **Public libraries:** Larger libraries have sections devoted to business. Librarians are usually more than glad to support your research efforts. If a publication is only available online, often the library has a subscription.

- *Online:* Using Google to search the name of the profession or industry, the word association, and country. For instance: *Building Materials Association USA* or *Human Resource Management Association Canada.* Every profession and industry has at least one. Contact them. They will provide not only the name(s) of their publication(s), but also names and possible introductions to possible Connectors.

Authors of articles are often an untapped source of Graduate Advantage opportunities.

Face-to-face networking

Connecting opportunities can be divided into two broad categories: *spontaneous* and *planned.* Spontaneous networking can occur at bus stops, in fast-food lines, or anywhere people interact. Planned networking is usually characterized by a specific group event or an invitation.

Networking events don't have to use the word *networking* to qualify as a networking event. Any event which gives you the prospect to meet potential Connectors is a networking event.

You can find many good networking opportunities at most social events. These events can include family gatherings, weddings, neighborhood gatherings and religious services.

I have received feedback that some of the best Connectors were met at neighborhood events. One former student attributes the Santa Claus parade to helping her launch a very rewarding career. She met a Connector at the parade who introduced her to a hiring manager.

Business social events are usually plentiful if you know where to look. Your local Chamber of Commerce can provide you with a list of upcoming events and appropriate contacts. Most alumni have regional chapters, which can offer some great networking possibilities.

Two other sources of networking opportunities are industry and professional association meetings and conferences. Both are usually open to "invited guests." Invitations are usually obtained by contacting the person designated for memberships on their website.

How often you can attend meetings for free is up to the discretion of the association. From feedback I've received, as long as you are unemployed and conduct yourself professionally, a time limit is not usually imposed.

Often conferences need volunteers for a variety of duties. By volunteering, you'll receive free admission. These are goldmines of opportunities.

Never take your resume with you. *Period.* If someone asks you for a copy of your resume, ask them for their business card. This will give you time to research the individual and company.

Another source of networking opportunities is meetups. Simply put "meetups [your city name]" into Google's search engine. Depending on your community size, there should be a list of groups. Even if there aren't any events relating to your field of interest, choose a few to go to anyway. These are great places to practice your first impressions and your interpersonal skills.

From a time perspective, business-type networking events will often seem to be the best source of Connectors. However, many graduates have found that spontaneous and social networking actually generates the most Connectors.

Reaching out by sending emails

The most common and acceptable way to connect with potential Connectors in non-face-to-face situations is through email. Today everyone is inundated with emails, many of which are spam. So the chances of your request being read and responded to can be slim.

To increase your response rate, consider the following: If you have or can obtain the person's business phone number, call them when they are least likely to answer, for example, Saturday evening. You don't want to speak to them, just leave a message. Simply identify who you are, acknowledge they probably don't have time to read every email. Therefore you are taking the liberty to tell them they will be receiving an email from you. Briefly summarize the contents, including subject line, and say you look forward to their response.

Short, professional, and to the point are the characteristics of effective emails requesting information and/or Graduate Advantage opportunities. Your subject line should be to the point; i.e., "Recent graduate seeks assistance." If someone referred you, mention this; for example, "John Smith suggested I contact you," or "I'm a John Smith referral."

Here is a possible template to consider using.

- First, your opening salutation is formal: Dear Mr./Ms/Dr. _____.

- The body: aim to keep it to no more than 90 words.

  State who you are and why you are reaching out to them. For instance: My name is John Smith and I just graduated from _____. I learned about you from your LinkedIn profile; or, from _____ alumni database; or, in speaking with Jane Jones she recommended you would be a good person to speak to.

  I would appreciate 15 minutes of your time, at your convenience, to learn more about working in the _____ field.

- Your closing will depend on whether you left a phone message. If you did, simply end with "Thank you for taking the time to consider my request" or "Looking forward to hearing from you at your convenience." If there was no pre-email phone message, close with what you are going to do. For instance: "Thank you for your time. I will contact you next week."

If the potential Connector after receiving your phone message and follow-up email doesn't respond within a week after receiving your email, chances are slim they will respond at all. That said, clients have told me that to their surprise, and mine, they have received replies weeks—and in one case, months—after they sent their email and left their phone message.

If you didn't use the pre-email phone strategy, wait two weeks and follow up with another email. State you understand how busy they are and that they may possibly have accidentally deleted your message. Then restate your original email message. If still no response, move on.

When your response rate is low, consider this alternative: Use snail mail. Remember to use resume-type paper. Make sure you use your full signature line.

Preparing to Leave Your Comfort Zone

Before you can confidently enter the world of face-to-face networking, you must master the following two subjects: the First Impression and the Mini Brand Bite.

We covered first impressions in the last section. First impressions are vital to your success, so if you skimmed that part, please go back and read it now.

Mini Brand Bites

Tradition says you need an elevator pitch to effectively network. An elevator pitch is a 30-second-to-2-minute verbal monologue. Supposedly, the term comes from a scenario of accidentally meeting someone important in an elevator. You have 30 seconds to 2 minutes to convince the person you have something important to say. If successful, the important person agrees to meet you to learn more.

If you are on an elevator with someone important for more than 30 seconds, the elevator pitch might work. More than likely, you will be in a room filled with people who are anxious to give you their pitch or talk about whatever interests them. Take it from me, after listening to dozens of elevator pitches your brain goes numb. Or at least mine does.

Here's the problem. Research indicates that most people's attention span is between 8 to 20 seconds. Couple this with the fact people generally remember only a few words you said. The chances of being remembered in a positive way are not high.

Let's approach networking interactions from a different perspective: The **Mini Brand Bite** approach. The idea is to share information about yourself in a focused, conversational manner. These bites can be easily modified to any conversational circumstances. The goal is more about getting people to like you than remembering what you said. If people like you, you have a better chance of developing a professional relationship, which is the goal of networking.

Let's look at one possible scenario. After you have "anchored" yourself, introduce yourself, create interest and ask an opened ended question. It might look like this:

"Hi, my name is James Williams. To my surprise, I recently graduated from Columbia University. (Mini brand bite:) *How did you get started in your career?"*

The individual now has a choice about how to respond. They can either ask you what you mean by "to my surprise," or they can share with you how they got started.

If they ask you what you mean by "to my surprise," you can respond with something like:

"It wasn't until I discovered my interest in environmental biology that I was committed to completing my degree. I have a natural ability to connect with people from all walks of life. (Mini brand bite:) *Do you have any suggestions about what type of work I should be looking for?"* (or: *"I'm interested in learning about what it's like to work in the _____ field, do you know of anyone I can speak to about this?"*)

They will possibly ask you more questions before they venture any suggestions about type of work, etc. By answering these questions, you will have provided another mini brand bite.

If, instead, they decide to share how they got started, *listen.* They might be sharing some important information. Also, by showing genuine interest you are building a possible Connector relationship.

Spontaneous Networking

These opportunities are by far the most challenging. From ski lifts to airline check in lines, opportunities can appear from nowhere. You have to be ready. At first, starting conversations with strangers, particularly older people, will take you out of your comfort zone. The following generic script can be modified to any situation:

- First, hit your anchor button and mentally review what your body language is saying before you say anything.

- Then verbally establish common ground with something like, "How is your day going?"

- If the person responds positively and then asks you how your day is going, see this as a green light to proceed. Say something like, "Thanks for asking. I am so happy I just graduated from _____. I'm trying to learn what it is like to work in the _____ field. Would you know off the top of your head anyone I could speak to about this?"

- The person may suggest someone to speak to, in which case you quickly retrieve a business card and pen. Remember to ask for their name (you need to say who is referring you).

- On the other hand, if the person sincerely can't think of anyone, offer your business card. Write your field of interest on the front of your card. Don't be afraid to ask for the contact's business card.

Be prepared to move onto the next person if the current one doesn't indicate any interest in continuing the conversation.

Don't decide whether to start or not start a conversation based on what a person is wearing. People have told me amazing stories about establishing rewarding relationships with people who weren't looking their professional best when they first met them.

Planned Networking

These events are usually more predictable.

Especially when starting your networking lifestyle, just getting up the nerve to walk into a room full of strangers is a major accomplishment. You know you are stepping out of your comfort zone.

Often the first priority when entering a room is to decide to whom you should speak. Top candidates are individuals not engaged in a conversation or otherwise preoccupied (i.e. texting). Check around the periphery of the room to see if anyone is either seated or standing by themselves. People lined up or standing around the hors d'oeuvres table, if there is one, can be another source of networking candidates.

Having a goal before entering a networking event helps you pace yourself and stay focused. Make sure your goal puts you outside your comfort zone. For instance, you might set a goal of getting three names to contact about your field of interest.

As your confidence grows, set higher goals. Be careful not to focus solely on a number at the exclusion of building quality relationships.

You will learn that not every networking event will be a success. Quite frankly, some will be duds. What makes bad events good is that you really appreciate the good ones.

Even after attending only a few events, you will notice a marked increase in your self-confidence as you push your comfort zone boundary.

Don't Forget the Paperwork

The easiest thing to forget is to send a simple thank-you. Not doing this destroys a budding professional relationship. As a general rule, for every business card you acquire, follow up with a thank-you email within 12 hours. For instance:

Hi, _____.

Enjoyed our conversation last night, particularly your thoughts on _____. As mentioned last night, I am interested in learning more about what it's like to work in the _____ field.

(Your online signature)

Connecting to a Graduate Advantage

Your chances of obtaining a Graduate Advantage are greatly increased if you have been referred. For instance, in response to your question about wanting to learn more about what it's like to work in the Transportation Management field, an individual suggests you speak to his sister-law who works in this field. Now this individual has become a Connector.

You immediately do three things:

1. On the back of one of your business cards, write down the sister-in-law's name, ensuring proper spelling, along with her company, contact information (phone and email).

2. Exchange business cards.

3. Ask your Connector

    a. what's the best way to reach the sister-in-law, and

    b. to give the sister-in-law a heads up you will be contacting her.

Within 12 hours, email your Connector, thanking them for the referral. Mention how excited you are to be speaking with a Supply Chain Management professional.

Now wait at least two days before trying to reach out to the sister-in-law. This will give you time to research the sister-in-law and her employer. This will also give the Connector time to touch base with his sister-in-law and time for both to Google your name and at least read your LinkedIn profile.

Follow your Connector's suggestion about contacting his sister-in-law. The following are two generic scripts to be modified to your circumstances:

Phone

Hi, Ms _____. Thanks for taking my call.

My name is _____. I had the opportunity to speak with your brother-in-law, _____, recently. He suggested you might be able to help me. I just graduated from _____ with a major in Supply Chain Management.

I would like to learn what's it's really like to work in this field. I would really appreciate a 15-minute meeting at your convenience. We could do it over coffee if that works best for you. Would later this week or next work best for you?

Email

Dear Ms_____,

I am a new graduate from _____ with a major in Supply Chain Management.

I recently had the opportunity to meet your brother-in-law, _____. After I explained my interest in learning what's it's like to work in the Supply Chain Management field, he suggested I speak to you.

I would appreciate a 15-minute meeting with you at your convenience. Looking forward to hearing from you.

(Your online signature)

Discovering Graduate Advantage opportunities is often referred to as the numbers game. This means the more contacts you convert to Connectors, who in turn generate Career Advantage opportunities, the better your chances of obtaining career opportunity interviews.

Every sales executive learns this very simple and powerful concept early in their career: **The more people you speak to, the more sales you generate.**

For instance, let's say you start with 100 contacts. You convert these contacts to 35 Connectors who help you obtain 5 Graduate Advantage opportunities. Using these numbers as an example, if you want 10 Graduate Advantage opportunities you need to start with 200 contacts.

The following visual illustration will help explain this idea:

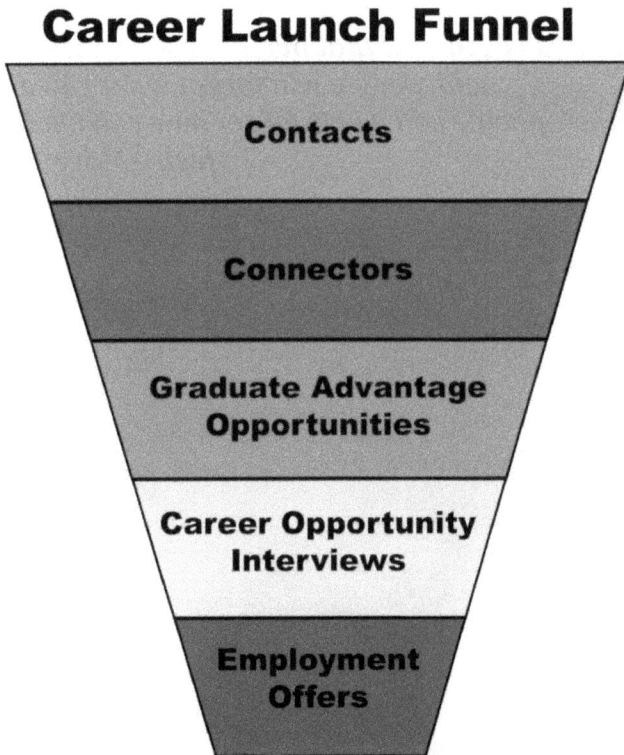

Career Launch Funnel

Contacts

Connectors

Graduate Advantage Opportunities

Career Opportunity Interviews

Employment Offers

Now you understand how to access Graduate Advantage opportunities. To quote the Nike slogan, "Just Do It!"

Action is the foundational key to all success.
~ Pablo Picasso

I've learned that people will forget what you said, people will forget what you did, but people will never forget how you made them feel. ~ Mayo Angelou

SECTION 6:
Following Your Resume In

Questions to Consider

1. What important information does a position description give you?

2. Why are positions on job boards considered fools' gold?

There might be times when you see or hear about a position without a referral. For instance, you might be reading a professional journal, see a job ad, and immediately think the job has your name on it.

Thoroughly check your Connector network to see if anyone will be able to help you.

You don't want to apply until you have more information about the position. The best source of information is the company's position description. You need to ask for a copy. Obtaining a copy of the position description helps give you a possible inside track on the applicant assessment process. How you approach a company can determine how cooperative they will be in providing a position description.

First, check to see if the position is advertised elsewhere. You might discover it is advertised on the company's LinkedIn page as well as on a job board aggregator such as Indeed (www.indeed.com) or SimplyHired (www.simplyhired.com)

Your best option is phoning the person identified in the ad. Ask for a copy of the position description and start building a professional relationship.

On the other hand, if the position is only advertised on a job board, reaching out to anyone in the organization can be challenging. Your best chance of making a connection is try to identify possible employees on LinkedIn.

Position Description—What's In It For You

A position description can also be called a job description or a position profile. The primary purpose is to identify the objective and the key responsibilities of a given position.

As a general rule, the larger and more established an organization, the more comprehensive their position descriptions are. These descriptions usually cover title, duties, purpose, responsibilities, scope, compensation range, working conditions, skills, and qualifications. These documents can be 3 pages or longer.

Smaller organizations tend to focus on listing the title, key responsibilities and desirable qualifications. These are usually a one pager.

Job ads are usually summaries of position descriptions. Sometimes companies use the full position description as an ad. They simply cut and paste.

Position descriptions are often used as a source for interview questions.

Regardless of the length and depth of a position description, there will be a list of action verbs which are usually skills. These can usually be found under the heading of duties and responsibilities.

Make a list of these action verbs/skills. If they aren't part of your transferable skill group, check to see if these can be found in your skills synonyms. The idea is to connect your skills back to the ones identified in the ad and vice versa.

You can use these skills or their synonyms in your covering letter and resume to build the connection.

Position descriptions can become outdated fairly quickly in organizations which are growing or going through major changes. This is evident when there is a difference between what an ad says and what the position description says.

The Truth Is: Your Chances Are Slim

Although you might see a job posted on a job board, realize that, in all likelihood, hundreds of resumes have been submitted within the first hour.

Certainly try to obtain a position description, but don't get your hopes up. My advice is not to spend too much time crafting your covering letter and resume. If the organization is within your geographical area, consider delivering a paper copy of your covering letter and resume. However, realize that once a vacant position is made public, organizations will usually only accept applications electronically.

In my opinion, job board ads are fools' gold. You can get "really busy" applying to job ads. This only creates a false sense of accomplishment. In the end you have accomplished nothing.

From feedback I've received, applying for positions in this hyper-competitive job market without a connector advocating for you can be a waste of time.

Working on the right thing is probably
more important than working hard.
~ Caterina Fake

You have to do what you dream of doing even while you're afraid. ~ Arianna Huffington

Pre-interview

Questions to Consider

1. Is salary really what it is all about?

2. What do you not know that can hurt you?

3. What questions are you afraid an interviewer *might ask*?

You have been offered a career opportunity interview. After you have finished doing your happy dance, you need to start preparing.

Ask the person who set up the interview for a copy of the position description. If a copy is available, they will usually provide one.

You need to accomplish the following pre-interview actions before you will be ready to meet the interviewer.

Understand the Position

Section 6 explained how to identify the skills, action verbs and their synonyms found in the position description and any posted ads. Study these documents until you feel you have a solid understanding of the position. The best way to do this is to practice answering the interview question, "Please describe your understanding of the position." You should see a connection between the skills and synonyms used in the ad and the position description.

Understand the Interviewer, the Company and the Industry

Start gathering information about the interviewer(s), the company and the industry. While doing Graduate Advantages, you have mastered the fundamentals of research. Now you have to dig deeper.

Learning about your interviewer(s) shouldn't be difficult. The interviewer's LinkedIn profile is a good place to start. By Googling the person's name, you should be able to add to your understanding of who the interviewer is. You are looking for a common interest. This can range from attending the same school, being fans of the same teams, or having interest in the same hobbies. On the other hand, your professionalism and preparedness can more than make up for any lack of common interest.

If for any reason the interviewer's name doesn't show up in your search, consider this a big red flag. Red means stop. I highly recommend you politely decline or just not show up. In today's internet-based world you have to intentionally want to hide so as not to be found. (However, keep in mind that this does not apply to individuals whose position would require they keep a low profile for security reasons.)

One of the interview questions often asked is, "What do you know about us?" Providing information easily found on the company website and LinkedIn page is a good start. Become familiar with the company's products and services. If possible, know a bit of the company history and the names of the President/CEO. In your Graduate Advantages, you may have picked up an interesting nugget. Check with your connections network to see if anyone has some inside knowledge. Search the internet for something positively noteworthy. The more knowledgeable you are, the more confident you are going to be.

Feedback I have received suggests that if you are being interviewed by the company's owner or president, particularly of smaller organizations, expect to demonstrate a solid understanding of the company and their industry. If it's a small start-up company, chances are information might be limited. In this case, a thorough knowledge of the industry is a must.

For entry-level positions, the interviewer(s) generally doesn't expect you to have a comprehensive knowledge of the company's industry. Being able to quote some easily found facts is sufficient. However, if you are applying for marketing and sales positions, more research is required.

Consider Compensation

Now is the time to research the compensation issue. Compensation is a broad term. It is divided into three categories. These are *direct financial, indirect financial* and *non-financial* compensation.

Direct financial refers to what employer pays you for your labor. This includes wages, salaries, bonuses and commissions.

Indirect financial refers to all monies paid out to an employee which are not included in direct financial compensation, such as benefits, retirement plans and paid leaves of absences.

Non-financial compensation doesn't have any monetary value. This can include achievement rewards, paid training, prizes and job satisfaction.

Sites like Glassdoor (www.glassdoor.com) can provide meaningful salary averages. Contacting professional associations and regional economic development agencies can add to your understanding.

You need to know what the realistic entry-level salary range is for an organization subject to industry, size and geographical location.

Direct compensation is important. Chances are, if your direct financial needs are not being adequately met, the other two forms of compensation usually don't hold much value. I intentionally use the word "usually" because one of the most important benefits of your first job is having a supportive manager. A boss who wants to see you get off on the right foot can help set the stage for your future success. Your manager can provide much needed mentoring. Sometimes you have to find a balance between direct financial compensation—that is, salary—and non-financial compensation—a great boss.

Careers are built on relationships, not on salaries.

Many successful people will tell you how their first boss had a profound effect on their careers.

Know What Attire is Appropriate

When you are in contact about the position description, ask about dress code or what the appropriate attire is for an interview. Why not wear what they suggest? Your Graduate Advantage experience may have been an excellent source of appropriate attire ideas. This is also a good time to review the "attire" portion of the the Preparation section.

Remember: Before an interviewer even shakes your hand, they already have an impression of you from what you are wearing.

Rehearse Your Interview

Using your video recorder, start practicing your interview answers (see the questions in the next section). Consider attaching pictures of the people who are going to interview you under the lens of your video recorder. You can use a picture from their LinkedIn profile or any other professional posting. Practicing speaking to the person(s) who is going to interview you adds a new dimension of realism to your practice.

Be Prepared—Small Details Count

- From your Graduate Advantage experiences, you know the importance of checking travel times or Skype connections.

- Remember to put several copies of your printed resume in your portfolio as well as a copy of the position description.

- By now you can see how important your Graduate Advantage experience has been in preparing you for the real thing.

What you do today can improve all your
tomorrows. ~ Ralph Marston

The Interview

Questions to Consider

1. Are you ready?

2. How do you pronounce the interviewer's name(s)?

3. What are two questions you must ask before the end of the interview?

Remember: Your only job is to make the interviewer's job easy.

For most graduates, job interviews are a daunting experience. They are a forced leap out of their comfort zone. The big difference between you and most graduates is you have mastered the Graduate Advantage. You are not blindly leaping, hoping for the best. You are confidently stepping up to the next level in your career-launch program.

It's not the most qualified who gets the job; rather, ***it's the one who is most prepared.***

The actual interview is a culmination of two processes. The first process was started with your decision to launch your career. The second process started when a potential employer put your name into a search engine.

From the Interviewer's Perspective

There is no such thing as a typical interviewer. Interviewers can be senior managers, junior recruiters, company owners, managers or just about anyone else assigned to the role of interviewing. Some have extensive formal interview training and years of experience. Others bring nothing to the table but the desire to learn. In fact, you could be the first person they ever interviewed. Interviewers can be classic introverts or very charismatic or somewhere in between.

The smaller the organization, the less likely they are to have a designated human resources (HR) person to handle interviewing. Usually the owner or a key manager in a small business is tasked with interviewing.

As a general rule, the larger the organization, the greater the probability the interviewer will have some formal interview training.

Some interviewers let their personality show through, often for rapport building purposes. They are relaxed and good conversationalists. On the other end of the scale, some interviewers dogmatically stick to an interview script. You can feel their tension. They are the ones who can make an interview feel like an interrogation. In the end you have to be prepared for whatever type of interviewer you meet.

> *Life is 10% what happens to you and 90% how you react to it. ~ Charles Swindoll*

What interviewers have in common is that at any given moment they are juggling multiple priorities. They aren't going to invest their valuable time interviewing you unless they see some potential. Your job is to make sure their investment pays off.

Making a hiring recommendation or decision carries two interrelated risks which experienced interviewers want to mitigate. First, the cost of a wrong hire can be staggering. *Conservative estimates put the direct cost of a wrong hire as 30% of an individual's first year's earnings.* This does not include indirect costs such as lost productivity and impact on employee morale. The second risk is interviews have less than on an average a 50% chance of predicting subsequent job success.

A person's ability to identify successful employees often carries career advancement implications. If a manager hires the wrong candidate, the manager's career path could become restricted. On the other hand, if a manager has the ability to pick "winners," that manager is often perceived as competent, with the potential for bigger and better things.

Experienced interviewers know that approximately 40% of all applicants (aka the 40 Percent Club) have supplied distorted information, have embellished information, and/or have omitted information in regards to their application. This includes everything from length of employment, job responsibilities, grades, accomplishments, or salaries to reasons for leaving organizations. Often, people don't realize providing false or misleading information can be grounds for termination.

From a business owner's perspective, hiring the wrong people can quickly destroy their company.

HR people know all too well the damage a bad hire can do.

Over the years, I have developed my own red flag warning system when interviewing. This has protected me many times from supporting, recommending, and/or hiring the wrong candidate. Red flags for me are candidates who:

- wear inappropriate attire;

- have poor personal grooming;

- blow the first impression opportunity;

- show incongruence between the covering letter, resume and LinkedIn profile;

- are not prepared for questions;

- provide shallow, rote answers that are easily found on the internet;

- have no questions or very shallow questions;

- refuse to or are unable to make eye contact;

- demonstrate differences between verbal and non-verbal communication;

- disagree often or are confrontational;
- are unable to explain or support information on the resume or LinkedIn profile;
- cause my gut to tell me that this person might belong to the 40 Percent Club.

About Interview Questions

Because you have done at least a few face-to-face Graduate Advantages, you understand the process. The two big differences between Graduate Advantages and career opportunity interviews are the length of the interview, and the fact that now someone else is asking the questions.

Although there are hundreds of possible interview questions asked in a variety of ways, the interviewer is usually trying to find the answers to three fundamental questions.

The three fundamental questions are:

1. Can you do the job?
2. Will you do the job?
3. Will you fit in?

"Can you do the job?" is fairly easy to answer if a candidate has a work history. By looking at a candidate's previous experience, asking enough of the right questions, and doing some solid reference checking, a skilled interviewer is usually able to answer the question with a certain degree of confidence.

For recent graduates this can be more difficult, but it's by no means impossible. Although you don't usually have much related previous experience, you have your transferable skills. As well, you possibly have volunteer, summer, part time and intern experience to demonstrate how you have used your skills.

"Will you do the job?" is a more difficult question. It's about motivation, a work ethic and commitment to see a task through. The

best way to answer this is with examples of what has motivated you, how a proven work ethic is part of your value system, and how tenacious you are about achieving your goals.

Lack of willingness to do the job is expressed in many ways. This can range from just doing the very bare minimum (aka the "walking dead") to not doing the work because of preoccupations. By far, texting and social media activities are the prime culprits. The bottom line is most employers won't tolerate an employee who takes a salary but doesn't do the work.

"Will you fit in?" is the million-dollar question. This is really a multifaceted question, and by far the most difficult one for interviewers to reach a comfort level with. This question is really asking:

- Can a solid professional employee-manager relationship be developed?

- Can the candidate become an effective team member?

- Can the candidate build relationships with other employees, suppliers and customers?

Building effective teams takes effort, time and money. Every time a new member is introduced, the team's equilibrium is jeopardized. As a candidate, you need to demonstrate through examples how you have adapted to new environments through flexibility and understanding other peoples' views. It's important to provide examples of how you have built relationships with people of different ages and cultures.

It's possible information from social media, references, background checks and psychological assessments may be used to supplement answers to the three questions.

A Glimpse of the Interview Process

The interview process has different stages, formats, delivery methods, phases and types. This means there can be a number of different combinations.

There are different stages in the process. These include the initial screening interview, general interview, and the follow up interview.

The purpose of the screening interview is to ensure a candidate meets the minimum requirements. The general interview is a thorough assessment of a candidate. This can include a series of interviews, one after another. The follow-up interview involves asking a candidate to return to confirm or clarify information or observations already made. Sometimes the different stages are rolled up into one interview.

Four basic interview formats

Interviews can take one of four formats:

1. one-on-one interviews,
2. serial interviews,
3. panel interviews, and
4. group interviews.

The **one-on-one interview** simply means you are interviewed by one person.

The **serial interview** is an extension of the one-on-one. You go from one interviewer to another interviewer. Organizations often want to gain the insights of various people, particularly when team cooperation is important.

When two or more individuals interview you at one time, this is referred to as a **panel interview**. These are often used in government and non-profit agencies.

Group interviews occur when several candidates are interviewed at the same time by at least one interviewer. These are by far the most intimidating, but they are rarely used for entry level positions.

With the advent of webcams and VoIP, another delivery method has been added. Prior to the advent of these technologies, interviews were conducted in person or by phone. Using a VoIP technology like Skype, you have the advantage of face-to-face interaction, without the hassle of travel. An interviewer in Los Angeles can interview candidates in Toronto, New York and London, all in the same day.

Four interview phases

The typical interview can be divided into four phases. These phases are:

1. the introduction;
2. the interviewer questions;
3. the candidate questions; and
4. the close.

The **introductory** phase consists of greetings and creating the important first impression.

The **interviewer** questions can be divided into three categories: *rapport building, specific questions*, and *clarification* questions.

As a **candidate**, your questions are your opportunity to gain a better understanding of the position.

The **closing** is about you expressing your interest and asking what the next step is.

Interviewer Questions

By far the largest portion of your time spent launching your career will be preparing and practicing your answers to interview questions. There are no short cuts to developing authentic answers and delivering them professionally.

This section covers different types of questions. Examples of how to create answers is provided for three types of questions. Use these as models to create your own answers. They are the Situational, Traditional, and Behavioral Interview questions. Lists of the three types of questions are provided in the Appendices VIII, IX and X.

It's important to start working on the answers as soon as possible.

For each question, use a separate Evernote note (or similar app) to develop your answer. At first, you might search the internet for rote answers to these questions. These answers can sometimes be a good beginning. Keep in mind that the interviewer has probably heard them many times before. You lose credibility very quickly when you provide the same memorized answers as everyone else.

As you start learning about yourself and conducting Graduate Advantages, you will notice your answers evolving. They will move from short, contrived responses to confident authentic answers.

Being able to deliver your answers professionally takes practice. There are no short cuts to getting it right. The easy part is memorizing your answers. The difficult part is delivering them with ease. As you know, face to face communication consists of three parts: what you say, how you say it, and your body language. The best way and only effective way to practice is to video record yourself delivering your answers. By recording yourself, you will be able see yourself as an interviewer sees you. This activity can often be a real educational experience.

It's easy to be overwhelmed by the number of questions to prepare answers for. Choose the ones you consider to be a cinch. Aim to work on 10 questions a day.

It's true you can't anticipate every interview question. However, what does happen is referred to as response generalization. You have easy access to so much information in the form of prepared answers. Your brain will pull together a quilt-type response to an unprepared question. A quilt is a group of partial ideas from various rehearsed answers integrated into a viable response.

Types of Interview Questions

Interview questions can be sorted into five types. While some are easier to navigate than others, your research and practice will help you put your best foot forward regardless.

Unstructured Interview Questions

Here, the interviewer doesn't have any prepared questions or sense of direction and it shows. The questions are often nebulous. Sometimes the interview seems more like a conversation. Other times, the interviewer jumps from subject to subject. There are no two interviews which are the same. If there are illegal or inappropriate questions, these are usually asked from a point of ignorance. Often the interviewer was "voluntold" to interview candidates. Sometimes the owner knows they need to add staff and they give interviewing their best shot.

It's difficult to provide examples of the type of interview questions you'll face in an unstructured interview, as the possibilities are immense. Sometimes, usually by accident, they will ask a situational, traditional or behavioral type question.

Often the interview is peppered with closed-ended questions, ones that are answered with a simple yes or no.

Preparing for this type of interview is next to impossible. However, if you have prepared for the other types of interview questions you should be able to handle most questions. The real advantage for the prepared candidate is you can take charge. Someone has to steer the direction of the conversation so it might as well be you.

Situational Interview Questions

These types of questions are often referred to as hypothetical interview questions. Situational interview questions ask you to envision and hypothesize how you would handle a particular situation if it were to arise. These questions usually involve problem solving, handling difficult situations, and making things happen in the workplace.

Situational interview questions are often a graduate's Achilles heel. unprepared for the question, the graduate "wings it." The answer, from an interviewer's perspective, can at times seem weak and possibly inapplicable.

Situational questions often start with phrases like

- Imagine if ... ?
- What would be your response to ... ?
- How would you handle ... ?

Examples of situational questions include

- Imagine you have a deadline and you are running out of time. What would you do?
- If your supervisor made a decision you did not agree with, how would you handle this?
- How would you deal with a colleague at work with whom you seem to be unable to build a successful relationship?

Although this type of question is future-focused, there is no reason you can't use past experiences to illustrate your point. In other words, move from a theoretical position to real life examples. The following steps offer a method for organizing your answers:

1. Identify (whenever possible) an experience from your past related to the situation or event which the question is posing.
2. Describe how you approached the situation.
3. Describe the outcome.

Examples

The following are two examples which illustrate moving from a theoretical position to using real life examples.

1. *If your supervisor made a decision you did not agree with, how would you handle this?*

   Your answer:

   Disagreements often arise from seeing the same issue from different perspectives. I think it's important to approach these types of situations with an open mind.

   Not agreeing with a decision has occurred twice in the last few years. The first was with my volleyball coach and the other was with a professor.

My volleyball coach wanted me to play a different position and the professor gave me a grade I didn't agree with.

The first thing I did was try to understand how and why they made their decisions. I think it's important to see things from the other person's point of view. I reviewed everything I might have done to support them arriving at their decisions. I believe Stephen Covey said in his book The Seven Habits of Highly Effective People *to seek first to understand, then to be understood.*

I mentally reviewed why I disagreed. I then asked to meet with each of them. I explained in a very non-confrontational manner that I didn't agree with the decision. I listened carefully to each one and understood where the person was coming from.

The coach and I agreed I would try the new position for the next five games. If the team's game didn't improve, I could go back to my old position.

The professor agreed to review my grade. However, after the review, he said he was not prepared to adjust it. I was okay with this because I was treated fairly.

I think being able to understand how a decision is made makes the decision more palatable.

2.   *How would you deal with a colleague at work with whom you seem to be unable to build a successful relationship?*

Your answer:

Outside of our professional lives we can choose who we build relationships with. In our professional lives, we often don't have a choice. Sometimes we have to work at it.

This situation occurred at my third summer job. I was assigned to work with another summer individual. We had to work as a team.

From the beginning, we just didn't seem to click as a team. He was non-communicative. This was impacting our ability to get the work done. Our supervisor commented that he thought we could be a lot more productive.

At first I was frustrated. Then I started wondering what role I could play in improving our relationship.

I waited until we were alone and not busy. I asked him in a casual friendly tone if we could have a chat. He nodded OK. I said I didn't think we seem to be getting along. I asked if I had said or done anything to offend him. I also mentioned it was important to me to have a good relationship with him.

He seemed to 'um' and 'er'. I could tell he was uncomfortable so I ended our conversation with "if anything comes to mind on how I could help improve our relationship I would appreciate hearing about it."

Nothing happened for a few days. Then he approached me and asked if we could have a chat. He said he had thought about our conversation. He shared the fact this was his first real work experience and he didn't know what to expect. He said from his perspective I was very confident and always seemed to know what to do. In fact he said he felt intimidated. Considering my work experience I could see how my confidence and knowledge could be interpreted as 'a know it all' attitude. I shared with him how overwhelmed I felt when I started my first job. We started understanding where each other was coming from.

The result of our conversation started an improvement in our relationship. Just being aware how I was being perceived helped me change. I think my co-worker became a bit more relaxed and open when he realized I had had the same feeling on my first job as he was experiencing.'

I believe if you can improve communications you have a good chance of improving a relationship.

See Appendix VIII for a list of situational interview questions.

Traditional Interview Questions

Traditional interview questions focus on your personality, education, goals, attitudes, personal interests, beliefs and preferred ways of thinking.

These questions are broad in nature with no right or wrong answers.

Traditional interview questions are often interspersed with behavioral and situational questions. They are often used at the beginning of an interview to help develop rapport.

For instance, in the early part of the interview process I usually ask, "Can you share with me some areas of improvement you would like to work on?"

You would be surprised how many times I get the deer-in-the-headlights look. Answers like "Well, I guess I could improve my reading skills" or "Maybe I should smile more when I'm talking with strangers" or "I really just can't think of anything" strongly suggest lack of preparedness and self-awareness.

Traditional interview questions often start with:

- Tell me . . . ?
- What . . . ?
- Why . . . ?
- How . . . ?

You need to become familiar with as many traditional interview questions as possible and develop your appropriate responses.

The answers to numerous traditional interview questions can be found online. If you use the answers as a guide to develop your own answers, great. Unfortunately, some people short cut the process and just memorize the online answers. And it shows.

An experienced interviewer quickly picks up the incongruence between a candidate's answers to behavioral questions and traditional questions. If the interviewer decides to follow up on the candidate's online memorized answers, the discrepancies become evident.

At this point, the candidate has taken a major credibility hit. A candidate's chance of recovering their credibility is very slim.

Examples

The following are two examples to help you start preparing your answers.

1. *Tell me about yourself.*

   There are several variations to this question including "Describe yourself," "Who are you?" and "What would you like me to know about yourself?"

   The "Tell me about yourself" question is a perennial favorite. Often this question is used near the beginning of the interview. The quality of your answer can reinforce the strong first impression you created.

   From an interviewer's perspective, I want to learn about you. This is a golden opportunity to teach me some important things about you.

   Having asked this question thousands of times, I'm amazed at how many folks miss this opportunity to score points.

   The interviewer doesn't want your life story. However some people feel driven to share irrelevant and personal information.

   There is not a right or wrong answer. There are, however, levels of relevance which you determine.

   It helps to mentally reframe the question to why you're an ideal fit for the job.

   The following are suggested steps for forming a credible answer:

   - Review your Graduate Advantage notes relevant to this position applied for

- Underline skills identified in the position description and job ad.

- Fill in the blanks and modify until you feel comfortable this is you.

The following are possible answers to the "Tell me about yourself" question:

- *My strongest skills are ____, ____, and ____. These have served me well. For example . . . [provide two or three examples of when and where you used them].*

- *My ____ [e.g. drive] and ____ [e.g. commitment] to get things done is best illustrated by . . . [provide two examples].*

- *People often comment about [or: people often say about me] . . . [e.g. how easily I make friends and get along with everyone].*

Since there is a 99% chance you are going to be asked this question, there is no reason not to be fully prepared.

Remember, like every other answer, if you are not delivering it with confidence and enthusiasm you are sending the wrong message, regardless of the words you speak.

2. *What makes a good employee?*

Your answer:

This question has been on my mind for at least a year before I graduated. My answer to this question comes from three sources.

First, I had asked family members and friends who were in management and professional roles. Second, I did some on-line research. Third, my networking experience provided me with valuable insights.

In my opinion there are several attributes a good employee must have. These are:

- *A commitment to learning. Good employees must be life-*

> *long learners. This helps drive the constant need to improve and fuels curiosity.*

- *Adaptability. The world is constantly changing. Companies and individuals have to adapt to changing conditions and events. I think adaptability is both a skill and an attitude. Employees who can't or won't change are a detriment to themselves and their team*

- *Excellent interpersonal skills. These can make or break employees. They might be brilliant, but if they can't get along with other people they are their own worst enemies. Excellent interpersonal skills often ensure a good fit.*

- *An excitement about life. Employees who see life as an exciting adventure bring this to their work life. This attitude seems to fuel how they get their work done and how they relate to people in general.*

See Appendix IX for a list of common traditional interview questions.

Behavioral Interview Questions

This type of interview question is based on the assumption that the most accurate predictor of future behavior is recent past performance in a similar situation. This interview style requires candidates to relate stories and personal experiences about how they have handled challenges and problems in the past.

One of the main reasons for the effectiveness of behavioral questions is the difficulty for candidates to make up behavioral stories—how they actually successfully solved a problem. You must have behavioral stories to back up whatever you have said on your resume and LinkedIn profile. For every strength and skill you have identified, be prepared to illustrate how you used them in a behavioral question context.

Behavioral interview questions are often not questions at all but rather statements. For example:

- Tell me how you ...

- Describe a time when you ...

- Give me an example of ...

This is by far the most popular type of interview. Sometimes behavioral answers can be adapted to answer other types of questions.

The best way to master answering behavioral questions is to use the STAR method. It is an acronym for a specific situation, task, action and result.

- **Situation:** Describe the specific situation or problem that corresponds to the question you have been asked. Be sure to give enough detail for the interviewer to understand. This can be from any previous employment (part-time, summer, fulltime) internships, volunteering, school, sports and clubs.

- **Task:** Explain what your task was in relation to the situation. What goal were you working towards or what task needed to get done?

- **Action:** Describe the action(s) you took to address the situation or problem. Provide a suitable amount of detail. Avoid as much as possible what other people did. The focus needs to be on what *you* did. Use the word "I" (not "we") when describing the action(s).

- **Results:** What happened? How did the event end? What was accomplished? Don't be shy about taking credit for your behavior. When possible, make sure your answer contains multiple positive results.

The following two examples illustrate the STAR method.

1. *Describe the most difficult situation you ever faced.*

   Your answer:

   [Situation:] *By the end of my sophomore year, I realized I didn't know what I wanted to major in or even if I was in the right faculty. I wasn't sure what to do. My parents had said they were really proud of my academic choice. I was afraid of disappointing them. From a financial point of view, I didn't feel comfortable continuing to borrow money from my parents and accumulating more student loan debt.*

[Task:] *I had to figure out what to do before I entered my junior year.*

[Action:] *I sat down with my parents and explained my situation. They said they understood and would support whatever I decided to do. In fact, my Mom had been in a similar situation.*

[Action:] *I met with a counselor from student services. He helped me look at different options. He also put me in touch with several people who were already working in the field I was interested in.*

[Action:] *I learned this field was still probably a good fit for me. I also discovered there were several ways to prepare for entry into the field.*

[Action:] *I decided to take a year off from full time studies. One of the people I had met through my counselor helped me get a job in her company. I took a few evening courses which confirmed what I wanted to major in as well as what I wanted to do when I graduated.*

[Result:] *Now that I have graduated, I realize taking a year off was a good decision. I was able to confirm my career interests. I was able to realign my studies to where I wanted to go in life. Working for a year eased the financial burden. By working for a year I learned how to build relationships with people of different ages and cultures.*

2. *Tell me about a time you had a deadline and were running out of time. What did you do?"*

Your answer:

[Situation:] *In my senior year, I got the flu which put me in bed for nearly two weeks. I had meticulously planned out my studies for the whole term. Losing two weeks meant I was going to miss getting a major project in on time. Missing the deadline would affect not only my grade but also my G.P.A. As well, I was hoping to use the professor of this course as a reference.*

[Task:] *I needed to finish this project on time. I had to find a way to get it done.*

[Action:] *First, I reviewed my study plans for each course I was taking. I found that by adjusting the individual time schedules, I was able to find some time.*

[Action:] *Second, I took a look at my non-academic life. I explained my situation to my volleyball coach who agreed to let me attend only one practice a week until my project was completed.*

[Action:] *Third, I announced on social media my commitment to getting my project done. I said I hoped my friends would understand why I wouldn't be having much time for hanging out with them.*

[Result:] *The end result was not only did I get my project in on time, but the professor told me I got one of the highest marks in the class. On a personal level, I learned that when I put my mind to something I can get it done.*

See Appendix X for a list of common behavioral interview questions.

Fear-Generating Interview Questions

There are questions which evoke fear or anxiety just reading them. These questions can be from any of the previously mentioned four interview types, and they can be different for every individual.

Some "fear" questions recent graduates have shared with me are:

- "Why is your GPA so low?"
- "Why has it taken you more than four years to graduate?"
- "How does your major prepare you for this job?"
- "Do you think the money spent on your education was worth it and why?"

Remember, the acronym for fear is *false evidence appearing real.* The more you prepare and practice your answers, the more confident you will feel.

Summing up the types of interviews

In summary, think about your behaviors, performance, and accomplishments in situations from different skill perspectives. Almost everything you have done can be explained differently by emphasizing different skills.

If you are not sure if you answered a question satisfactorily, ask the interviewer, "Did I answer your question?" Sometimes just the look on the interviewer's face is a cue to ask this question.

An answer might look good on paper, but speaking the same answer can seem awkward and contrived. The solution is video record your answers. As you practice your answers you'll notice they naturally become fine-tuned.

Your Questions

Because of your Graduate Advantage experience, you are now back on familiar ground. You are now perhaps feeling more comfortable and confident.

Although the interviewer has stopped asking questions, they have not stopped evaluating you. Many new graduates feel the interview is over when the questions end. They stop thinking and acting like a professional. They lose their edge.

Asking intelligent questions is another opportunity to confirm your fit.

Usually near the end of an interview, the interviewer will ask if you have questions. I used to say, "I've been asking all the questions, now it's your turn."

If they don't ask if you have any questions, this can be interpreted in several different ways. It's possible you have had an unstructured interview which was more like a conversation during which time your questions were answered. Sometimes interviewers are running behind schedule and just don't have the time.

A few organizations see interviewing as a one-way street. This says something. Do you want to work for an organization whose underlying philosophy is "Our way or the highway?"

Regardless of how the interview ends, politely ask the last question, "What is the next step in the process, and what is the timeframe?"

When you are given the opportunity to ask your questions, how many should you ask? That depends on a number of factors, including time and responsiveness of the interviewer. Remember, your first goal is to confirm you are a viable candidate, as well as conveying respect your interviewer's time. A general rule is to have five well-prepared and questions. Be ready to choose your best three.

Asking questions just for the sake of asking questions can convey the wrong impression. It's better, after asking a few good questions, to end your question period on a high note. Say something to the effect you appreciate the information and time the interviewer has shared with you, and ask if it would be okay to make contact again if you have any further questions.

Watch your interviewer for signals. If the person checks their watch, seems impatient, answers your questions with a yes or no or responds curtly, move to your last question. Your Graduate Advantage experience will serve you well in assessing the situation.

Each question you ask must demonstrate your interest and knowledge. Questions you've found on the internet have the risk of sounding shallow. However, you have probably picked up some bits of information from your Graduate Advantage which you can use to add depth to your questions.

There are no "right questions." It depends on the situation. Properly researched and well-thought-out questions take time to create. Always try to use information you have learned from your Graduate Advantages.

Review your Graduate Advantage notes. This is a good place to start.

The following are some generic questions which you should modify. Avoid creating questions which require a yes or no answer.

- Please describe a typical day or week in the position.
- Why is this position vacant?
- What's the biggest challenge in this position?
- What's the most important thing the person taking this position will be expected to accomplish in the first 90 days?
- In what way is performance measured and reviewed for this position?
- What skills and education does someone need to have in order to be really successful in this position?
- I realize things are constantly changing. What changes do you foresee for this position?
- How would you describe the ideal candidate for this position?
- What can you tell me about this job that isn't in the job description?
- What sort of training is provided to learn this position?
- What typical responsibilities does someone assume after they have been promoted?
- What are the most important skills needed to do this job?
- What is the next step in this process, and what is the timeframe?

For illustration purposes, let's modify a few questions.

Please describe a typical week.

Modified: *From my research, a typical week consists of . . . . What else [or: what unusual] things can occur?" Or: "How has the typical work week changed over time?*

What the biggest challenge in this position?

> Modified: *I understand the biggest challenge of this position is . . . . What are some of the other challenges a person in this position might face?*

What skills and education does someone need to have to be successful in this position?

> Modified: *From my research, I understand an undergraduate degree and strong computer and communication skills are essential. What other skills do you think are important?*

It's important to ask the last question, "What is the next step in the process, and what is the timeframe?" Often the interviewer will tell you what it is.

On the hand, maybe the interviewer can't answer this question right now because other people need to be consulted, and/or there are still other candidates to be interviewed. If the answer is vague in terms of timeframe, casually ask the interviewer if it's okay to touch base in two weeks.

Illegal Questions

All jurisdictions in the United States, Canada and the United Kingdom have laws and regulations regarding employment hiring. I suggest you become familiar with them.

Most experienced interviewers are aware of taboo subjects. These usually include sexual orientation, age, race, nationality, color, citizenship, religion and marital status.

Often, inexperienced interviewers accidentally wander into the area of inappropriate and sometimes illegal questions. If you know an interviewer has crossed the line, you have three options:

1. If you feel it is possible the interviewer just didn't know they had crossed the line, answer the question. But before you answer, make a mild inquisitive look, implying "That's a strange question." Then make your answer short and to

the point. Usually the non-verbal inquisitive look alerts interviewers something has gone wrong. If another illegal question is asked, move to the next option or, if more appropriate, the last option.

2. Reframe or redirect the question. For instance, if the interviewer asks about your family, reframe the question and say, "Do you mean, am I available to travel on a regular basis?"

3. Depending on which approach you are most comfortable with, either:

    a. ask as politely as possible if the interviewer knows they are asking an illegal question; or

    b. state as politely as possible that you would prefer not to answer an illegal question.

Choosing option 3 might be best. However, realize in creating psychological distance you have limited the possibilities of the interview having a successful ending. The reality is, it is better to terminate a bad interview than try and make it work. Since the interviewer is representing the company, what does that say about the company?

If you ever get the feeling that something isn't right, just terminate the interview.

A Word about Psychological Assessments

To gain an additional perspective on a candidate, a company will sometimes request a candidate complete some kind of psychological assessment.

A lot of people have never completed an assessment. Therefore, they don't know what to expect.

There are many types of assessments available. The majority used in recruiting/human resources focus on understanding your personality. There are also others which assess your skills, integrity, interests, motivation and ability.

The assessments are another way of validating interview observations and self-reported information. Overall, interviews alone do not have a very high success rate.

By far the biggest mistake people make when taking assessments is trying to choose the response they think will project them in the best light. Trying to be something you are not usually doesn't end well.

Many assessments have been designed to identify incongruent responses. Sometimes this is referred to as the reliability factor. If a completed assessment exceeds a certain incongruent percentage, it is considered invalid. However, this is often interpreted as you trying to pretend to be someone you are not.

My advice: don't try to figure out the best answer. Your first response is usually your best response. Don't over think every question.

Some organizations request you complete assessments before they will entertain the idea of interviewing you. From my experience, candidates are usually asked to complete them after an interview. This can be interpreted as a sign the company is interested in you. If the assessment(s) support the interviewer's observations, another interview will often follow.

Salary Negotiations

At some point during the interview process there will be a conversation about salary. As a general rule, do not be the person who initiates the conversation.

Some interviewers don't want to waste their time, nor yours, going through an interview only to find out they aren't prepared to meet your salary expectations. So they bring up the salary discussion early in the interview. On the other hand, other interviewers want to feel comfortable you are a viable candidate before they initiate the conversation.

As part of the pre-interview preparation, you have researched salaries. Interviewers usually know what they are prepared to pay for an entry-level position. When I have asked about salary expectations, I have had graduates on occasion quote salary ranges of mid-level managers. To me this demonstrates unreal expectations based on no research. Essentially this ends the interview.

The best way to handle the interviewer's question about salary expectations is to say something to the effect of, "My research indicates the starting salaries for this type of position in this industry is $____ to $____. However, I understand internal equity can affect these numbers."

Internal equity basically means the more responsibilities a position has, the more it pays in relation to other positions in the organization. So if a department manager position pays $45,000–$50,000 and an entry-level position pays $30,000–$35,000, a candidate asking for a salary of $40,000 would throw a monkey wrench into the situation. This could be referred to as a career-limiting move.

After you make your salary statement, follow up with a question to the interviewer such as, "Is this in the same range you are comfortable with?"

Confidence and Enthusiasm

Confidence and enthusiasm show. Remember, often it's not what you say; it's how you say it. Frequently, when we are so focused on making sure we are saying the right thing, we forget to put any positive emotion into the message. Even an experienced professional can forget to control the emotional tone of their message in stressful situations; sometimes new graduates can do it quite naturally.

> *If you think you can or if you think you can't*
> *either way you are right. ~ Henry Ford*

The Other Conversation

In face-to-face conversations, including digital, two exchanges of information are happening. One is verbal and the other is non-verbal. In a previous section we discussed the communication model. This model says your communication is made up of 55%

body language, including appearance, 38% tonality—the confidence and enthusiasm with which you speak—and 7% is the actual words you speak.

Body language is a well-researched topic. This has been the subject of numerous books and articles. I suggest you spend some time becoming familiar with this subject. Not only will it improve your overall interview skills, but once mastered, it will serve in your career as well as other areas of your life.

Here are a few key points to keep in mind:

- Throughout the interview, maintain an open body position. This means legs are uncrossed, arms are open, and when applicable, palms are exposed.

- Sit up straight.

- Maintain eye contact without staring.

- Intermittently use a relaxed smile.

- Nod your head to indicate you are listening and you understand.

Right After the Interview

As soon as you get home, sit down and review the interview. While it is fresh in your mind, answer the following questions:

- What are the names and titles of the people who interviewed you, if you didn't get their business cards?

- What questions were you not prepared for?

- Which questions do you think you aced?

- How well do you think you did making the first impression?

- What did you notice about the interviewer's body language?

- What could you have done differently?

- How could you have been better prepared?

- Is there one question you need to redress in your thank-you note?

The interview isn't finished until the paperwork is done

Each person who interviewed you should receive a thank-you note. This is a must; it says you are a professional. Thank-you notes are brief, with no more than four paragraphs, and can be either emailed or snail mailed. If you are using snail mail, they can either be typed or handwritten.

These notes are the opportune time to answer an interview question which you didn't answer well originally. It can happen to anyone. You have memorized and practiced your answers. The interviewer asks you a question, and for some reason your mind goes blank. You fumble through it and move on.

In your thank-you note, simply say, "After leaving the interview, I realized I could have provided more information [or elaborated more fully] when you asked me about [or: in our conversation about] . . . ."

Try keeping your explanation to no more than three sentences. If necessary, keep rewriting it until you have no more than three sentences.

Unless there is some urgent reason to ensure the interviewer receives the note immediately, consider opting opt for snail mail. Use the same quality paper you used for your covering letter and resume. If your handwriting is more than just legible, consider writing it by hand.

Generally, a spell-checked and grammatically proofed typed letter works well.

If you do decide to use email, omit the email address until you have written and proofread your letter.

The following is a sample you can adapt to your situation. Needless to say, each thank-you note you write is customized.

Company name

Street address

Date

Dear Ms/Mr./Dr. ____,

Thank you for meeting with me this morning/afternoon to discuss the position of ____. I enjoyed our conversation, and I am very excited about the possibility of joining your team.

Our interview confirmed my research about ____ Company. It is a dynamic innovative organization that walks their talk about their employees being "their biggest and best asset."

After reviewing our conversation and the position description, I believe my skills and education are an excellent fit. As well, I feel I could learn a great deal from you and would certainly enjoy working with you.

Again, thank you for considering me for this exciting opportunity. The interview served to reinforce my strong interest in joining your team. If you have any questions, please don't hesitate to contact me.

Sincerely,

Then send another email to keep your referral in the loop.

Summary

A tremendous amount of material has been covered in this section. If you have been working on your interview question answers and video recording your practice sessions, you are probably finally getting the feeling things are coming together.

If you push through that feeling of being scared, that feeling of taking a risk, really amazing things can happen.
~ Marissa Mayer

SECTION 9:
After the Interview

Questions to Consider

1. Why are you different from most graduates?

2. What's the worst thing that can happen?

3. Did you think you would change that much?

Finally!

The phone rings. You recognize the number from the caller i.d. It's from the company who has "the perfect fit job" you interviewed for last week. Your heart starts pounding. You answer. It's the interviewer offering you the position.

Congratulations!

Most organizations follow up verbal offers with what is commonly referred to as a letter of offer. This document usually specifies the job title, starting date, salary, and supervisor's title. Sometimes they outline primary responsibilities and benefits.

Often small organizations are informal when it comes to extending employment offers. Sometimes the interviewer will call, extend a job offer and, assuming you accept, ask you to be at their office at a certain time and date. It's easy to forget everything you heard except the salary and the time and date of your first day at work. If this happens, it is recommended that you send the interviewer an email confirming your acceptance and briefly restating what you think the interviewer said.

After you have finished celebrating, there are things which need to be done before you start your new life.

Your successful career launch is, in part, because many people decided to help you. They didn't have to; they chose to. Some gave you their time, and others gave critical information. And some gave both.

Take the time to write to every single person who has contributed to your success, regardless of the size of their contribution. A handwritten thank you note on resume grade paper will go a long way to confirming they made the right decision to help you. This note says you are a professional.

These simple handwritten thank you notes will stand as a testimony to your character.

As you move forward on your chosen career path the relationships you started building during your career launch need to be cultivated. Successful careers are built on professional relationships.

The Biggest Mistake

The largest blunder anyone can make is to assume because they felt the interview was a slam-dunk they will just wait for the inevitable, the job offer.

It's possible as the interview was wrapping up the interviewer inferred, or so you thought, the job was yours. A lot of things can happen between the end of an interview and an expected job offer. Here are some of the things I've witnessed:

- A decision is made not to hire anyone but rather to divide up the responsibilities among existing employees.

- There has been a departmental reorganization and the vacant position has been dissolved.

- A hiring freeze has been implemented. This could be for a number of reasons.

- Budget cuts have been made. This is an everyday corporate reality.

- Another candidate appears who is an even better fit for the position.

- Nepotism—"It's not what you know, it's who you know."

- References and background checks don't support the candidate.

- The hiring manager is promoted or moves on. The hiring process starts over again.

- There are second thoughts about the candidate.

In reality, all that has often happened at the interview is that you have, in your opinion, done well.

Until you have a job offer, usually written, which you are prepared to accept, you are still unemployed.

A Steep Price

Being human, there is a tendency to optimistically believe after the interview your career is about to be launched. Therefore it's simply a matter of time before the job offer comes through. But days, weeks and sometimes a month or two can pass just waiting. When the job offer doesn't come through, it's an enormous blow.

The blow is threefold:

1. Precious time has been lost and can't be recovered.

2. This is emotionally devastating. It's like a hard punch to the stomach. It takes a while to recover. After all, your expectations about a great job have been destroyed.

3. You have lost focus. It takes time and energy to manage a full time career launch program. Starting from square one again is demoralizing.

Don't Take the Risk

Do yourself a big favor: don't take the risk of setting yourself up for a major disappointment. There is only one way to manage this risk. Treat an interview as an opportunity to practice your interview skills.

An interview is not "a do or die" situation. It's a learning experience. The more interviewing experiences you have, the more you improve.

Now, more than ever, stay focused. Line up other Graduate Advantages and continue participating in networking activities.

Your Reality

You are in a truly unique position. Most graduates would naturally by excited by the possibility of any employment offer. You are different.

You have taken the time to start to get to know yourself. Add to this knowledge you have gained from Graduate Advantage opportunities. Combining these factors with your interview experience, you probably have a good sense of whether the position is a good fit.

Graduates have told me about the sinking feeling in their stomach and sometimes a mini-anxiety attack when they realized there is no fit between their strengths, values, interests and that of the position. What do they do? There are two options:

1. Communicate to the interviewer, either verbally or in writing, your appreciation for their interest. Then, explain you do not wish to pursue the opportunity any further. This is being authentic. Continue setting up Graduate Advantage opportunities and engaging in networking activities.

2. Because of financial necessity, accept the idea you will have to take the position if it's offered. You are still in a good position. Why? Because you know the position isn't a good fit, you won't beat yourself up if things don't work out. It's still possible to pursue career launch activities while being employed.

You Are Now a Different Person

From working through this manual, you have changed. It couldn't be otherwise. You have learned about yourself and started to see yourself in a whole new way. Among other things, you have learned how to conduct yourself as a young professional. By consistently stepping out of your comfort zone you have redefined yourself. You have learned how to set and achieve goals. Building professional relationships is now something you are able to do. You can confidently maneuver the mysteries of the hiring process.

The sole purpose of this manual has been to prepare you to professionally present yourself to potential employers. It would be nice to believe that everyone who has diligently followed the steps explained in this manual will quickly find a good-fit career opportunity. In reality, this will take some people longer than others.

I am the first one to admit that it is easy to get discouraged after months of giving it your best and still being unemployed. Therefore I would like to close with these words from Calvin Coolidge:

> *Nothing in this world can take the place of persistence.*
> *Talent will not; nothing is more common than unsuccessful*
>   *men with talent.*
> *Genius will not; unrewarded genius is almost a proverb.*
> *Education will not; the world is full of educated derelicts.*
> *Persistence and determination alone are omnipotent.*

Namaste.

Appendices

Appendix I: VIA Character Strengths

Note: This form can be downloaded from the manual's website: www.fromeducatedtoemployed.com/the-forms/.

List your top 5 strengths, and provide 2 examples of how and where you have used each strength.

Strength 1:

Example 1

Example 2

Strength 2:

Example 1

Example 2

Strength 3:

Example 1

Example 2

Strength 4:

Example 1

Example 2

Strength 5:

Example 1

Example 2

Appendix II: O'Net Interest Summary

Note: This form can be downloaded from the manual's website: www.fromeducatedtoemployed.com/the-forms/.

Record your RIASEC score_____

1. List up to 5 occupations from your RIASEC score which interested you.

2. What were 2 key skills of each occupation?

3. What did you find interesting about each occupation?

Occupation 1:
    Skill 1

    Skill 2

    Interest

Occupation 2:
    Skill 1

    Skill 2

    Interest

Occupation 3:
    Skill 1

    Skill 2

    Interest

Occupation 4:
    Skill 1

    Skill 2

    Interest

Occupation 5:
    Skill 1

    Skill 2

    Interest

Appendix III: Personal Attribute List

Note: This form can be downloaded from the manual's website: www.fromeducatedtoemployed.com/the-forms/.

Ask everyone you know to identify six attributes which describe you by putting a checkmark beside them, and when they saw the attribute used. (Keep track on **Attribute Summary List, Appendix IV**.)

candid	challenging	charismatic	charitable
cheerful	circumspect	clever	compassionate
collaborative	committed	competent	communicative
compassionate	competitive	confident	concise
confident	considerate	conscientious	consistent
constructive	contemplative	cooperative	coordinated
curious	courteous	creative	decisive
dedicated	dependable	detailed	determined
devoted	diligent	direct	disciplined
driven	dynamic	eager	effective
efficient	eloquent	empathetic	empowered
encouraging	energetic	engaging	enterprising
entertaining	entrepreneurial	enthusiastic	excited
experienced	experimental	expressive	fair
flexible	focused	free-thinker	friendly
fun	generous	genius	generous
gentle	genuine	gifted	giving
goal-oriented	graceful	gracious	gregarious
happy	hardworking	healthy	helpful
honest	hopeful	humble	humorous

idealistic	imaginative	independent	industrious
influential	informative	innovative	inquisitive
intriguing	introspective	insightful	inspiring
intense	intuitive	involved	just
kind	knowledgeable	leader	lively
logical	loving	loyal	mature
methodical	meticulous	mindful	moderate
moral	motivated	natural	neat
nice	nurturing	obsessive	objective
observant	open-minded	opinionated	optimistic
orderly	organized	original	outgoing
passionate	patient	peaceful	perceptive
persistent	personable	persuasive	polite
positive	practical	pragmatic	precise
present	proactive	productive	professional
punctual	quirky	rational	realistic
receptive	reflective	relaxed	reliable
respectful	responsible	resourceful	results-oriented
risk-taker	self-aware	self-motivated	sensible
serious	shrewd	sincere	smart
straightforward	strategic	studious	successful
sympathetic	systematic	teacher	tenacious
thorough	tolerant	transparent	trustworthy
unconventional	understanding	unique	unselfish
unusual	valuable	venturesome	visionary
work-oriented	wise	witty	

Appendix IV: Attribute Summary List

Note: This form can be downloaded from the manual's website: www.fromeducatedtoemployed.com/the-forms/.

Identify the 6 attributes which received the most checks, and list 2 occasions where each attribute was evident.

Attribute 1:

    Occasion 1

    Occasion 2

Attribute 2:

    Occasion 1

    Occasion 2

Attribute 3:

    Occasion 1

    Occasion 2

Attribute 4:

    Occasion 1

    Occasion 2

Attribute 5:

    Occasion 1

    Occasion 2

Attribute 6:

    Occasion 1

    Occasion 2

Appendix V: 11 Transferable Skills Employers Require

Note: This form can be downloaded from the manual's website: www.fromeducatedtoemployed.com/the-forms/.

Provide 2 examples of a situation where you used each skill.

1. Communication skills

    verbal
       a)
       b)

    written
       a)
       b)

    listening
       a)
       b)

    non-verbal (body language)
       a)
       b)

2. Honesty/Integrity
       a)
       b)

3. Team Player
       a)
       b)

4. Initiative
       a)
       b)

5. Adaptability

    a)

    b)

6. Problem Solving (reasoning and creativity)

    a)

    b)

7. Interpersonal (getting along with others while getting the job done)

    a)

    b)

8. Strong Work Ethic

    a)

    b)

9. Organizational/Planning

    a)

    b)

10. Stress Management

    a)

    b)

11. Computer (email etiquette, spread sheets)

    a)

    b)

Appendix VI: Common Transferable Skills Exercise

Note: This form can be downloaded from the manual's website: www.fromeducatedtoemployed.com/the-forms/.

Instructions

1. Read over the list of common transferable skills (**Appendix VII**) several times.

2. Identify 15 of your strongest skills – not including 11 Transferable Skill Employers Require.

3. Identify one synonym for each skill.

4. List 2 examples when you used the skill.

Skill1:   Synonym:

    a)

    b)

Skill 2:   Synonym:

    a)

    b)

Skill 3:   Synonym:

    a)

    b)

Skill 4:   Synonym:

    a)

    b)

Skill 5:   Synonym:

    a)

    b)

Skill 6:   Synonym:

    a)

    b)

Skill 7:   Synonym:

    a)

    b)

Skill 8:   Synonym:

    a)

    b)

Skill 9:   Synonym:

    a)

    b)

Skill 10:   Synonym:

    a)

    b)

Skill 11:   Synonym:
   a)
   b)

Skill 12:   Synonym:
   a)
   b)

Skill 13:   Synonym:
   a)
   b)

Skill 14:   Synonym:
   a)
   b)

Skill 15:   Synonym:
   a)
   b)

Appendix VII: Common Transferable Skills

Note: This form can be downloaded from the manual's website: www.fromeducatedtoemployed.com/the-forms/.

Communication skills group:

articulating	describing	editing
explaining	expressing	facilitating
interviewing	interpreting	listening
negotiating	perceiving	persuading
proofreading	promoting	providing feedback
publicizing	reporting	selling
speaking	summarizing	telling
translating	understanding	verbalizing
writing		

Creative skills group:

acting	brainstorming	composing
conceptualizing	conducting	creating
designing	detailing	developing
displaying	dramatizing	expressing
envisioning	generating	illustrating
imagining	improving	inventing
modeling	organizing	painting
performing	photographing	printing
rendering	shaping	singing
sketching	symbolizing	writing

Human Relations (Helping and Teaching) skills group:

advising	conflict resolution	coping
consulting	counseling	empathizing
giving	helping	intervening
interviewing	instructing	mediating
mentoring	motivating	offering
reconcile	referring	rehabilitation
resolving	serving	sharing
supporting	tactfulness	teaching
tending	tutoring	

Managing skills group:

auditing	budgeting	calculating
consolidating	controlling	deciding
delegating	determining	enforcing
evaluating	financing	implementing
integrating	monitoring	purchasing
recommending	recruiting	scheduling
supervising	troubleshooting	

Appendix VIII: Situational Interview Questions

You disagree with the way your supervisor handled a problem. What would you do?

What would you do if the work of a subordinate or team member was not up to expectations?

If you believed your supervisor was wrong, how would you handle the situation?

A co-worker tells you in confidence that she plans to call in sick while actually taking a week's vacation. What would you do and why?

How would you handle a situation if you met resistance introducing a new idea to your team?

What would you do if the priorities on a project you were working on suddenly changed?

How would you deal with a colleague at work with whom you seem unable to build a successful working relationship ?

How would you react if a team member was not contributing towards a project?

How would you handle it if you believed strongly in a recommendation you made in a meeting, but most of your co-workers shot it down?

List the steps that you would take to make an important decision.

What would you do if you realized at deadline time that a project you wrote for your professor was not up to par?

What would you do if you disagreed with the way your supervisor said to handle a problem?

How would you respond to a customer who wasn't happy with a product or service?

Appendix IX: Traditional Interview Questions

Do you have any plans for further studies?

What have you learned from your mistakes?

How would your best friend describe you?

How do you personally define success?

In what type of work environment are you most comfortable?

What are your three most important values and why?

What do you see yourself doing five years from now?

What have you learned from your mistakes?

How would a person describe you after they have had a disagreement with you?

What do you think it takes to be successful in this field?

How well do you adapt to new situations?

What are your long range career objectives?

Why are you interested in this career field?

What's more important for you—the work itself or how much you get paid for it?

How do you go about solving a problem?

What are your strengths?

What makes you go an extra mile on a project?

How do you work as part of a team?

Why did you choose this particular school to study at?

What qualifications do you have that would make you successful in this career field?

Why did you apply to this position?

What are the attributes of a good leader?

How would you evaluate your ability to deal with conflict?

What strategies do you have to ensure a successful career?

Why did you choose to study _____?

What was the most important book you have read recently?

How do you work under pressure?

What are your weaknesses?

What do you know about our industry?

What have you accomplished that shows your willingness to work?

Why is your GPA not higher?

What motivates you?

What accomplishments have given you the most satisfaction and why?

What were your favorite classes? Why?

What subjects did you get the lowest marks in and why?

Why do you want to work in the _____ industry?

How much does money motivate you?

Why should I hire you?

How has your education prepared you for this job?

What do you know about our organization?

What is one of the hardest decisions you have ever had to make?

How is your academic performance an indication of how you will perform on the job?

Appendix X: Behavioral Interview Questions

Give me an example of an occasion when you used logic to solve a problem.

Describe a time you when you went above and beyond the call of duty.

Give me an example of how you handled your schedule when it was interrupted.

Describe a time when you were faced with problems at school that tested your coping skills. What did you do?

Tell me about a time when things didn't go according to plan.

Give me an example of a time you had to make a decision quickly.

Tell me about a project or assignment for which you needed strong analytical skills to do well.

Give me an example of two of your strengths, and situations where you used them.

Give me an example of two of your weaknesses (aka challenges, areas of improvement) and describe how you are managing them.

Give me an example of a significant goal you achieved. Explain why it was significant and how you achieved it.

Tell me about a time you had to persuade someone to accept your point of view.

Give me an example of how you contributed to a team goal.

Tell me about your studies. Why did you choose this program?

Describe a situation when you joined a new team or moved into a new environment.

Tell me about a time when you had a disagreement with someone. What was the outcome?

Give me an example of a difficult situation you handled.

Tell me about a time when you had several challenging projects with different priorities to manage.

Describe a situation where you had to solve a difficult problem. What was the outcome?

Tell me about a situation when you had to deal with a very upset person.

Provide me with an example of a situation when you didn't achieve a goal.

Tell me about a time when you had to do something you didn't necessarily agree with.

Tell me about a situation when you had to speak up in order to get a point across.

Tell me about a time you had too many things to do and how you prioritized them.

Describe a situation in which a detail you thought to be unimportant turned out to be very important.

Tell me about the most stressful situation you have ever been in. How did you handle it?

Give me an example of a time when you had to keep from speaking or making a decision because you did not have enough information.

Give me an example of when you showed initiative and took the lead.

Tell me about a time when you weren't pleased with your performance. What did you do about it?

Describe a situation where your team player skills shone.

Tell me about a time you felt particularly good about the results you were able to get on an assignment.

Give me an example of a situation where you worked under a tight deadline.

Describe your proudest achievement. Walk me through how you did this.

Describe a time when you received criticism.

Tell me about a time when you had to deal with a demanding person.

Tell me about a time you had put in extra effort to get the results you needed.

Tell me how you go about learning a new topic.

Describe a conflict you were involved in and how you resolved it.

Give me an example of a time when you went above and beyond the call of duty.

Learn More

Interested in staying up to date on the latest career launch tips and strategies? Or maybe you have a question. Join the book's Linkedin group.